Road Rage

Andrew Nicholson

To Mark & Jane
Enjoy the ride

Editor: Jennie Clague
Cover Design: Nina Reitan 2017
www.andrewnicholsonnz.wixsite.com/roadrage

ISBN: 978-0-473-38960-4

DEDICATION

For Warren

Contents

Acknowledgements

Firstly: Thanks to 'mission control team' who did more than simply organise. In addition to tackling logistics, you believed in me, kept my spirits up, tolerated my tantrums and my sometimes irrational behaviour. Thank you to my wife Marcela, Tanis from CTCR and my brother Chris. Particular thanks to Jennie who helped me before the ride, during the ride, with the application process and finally to publish this book. You easily saved me the scant 52 hours by which I broke the record, and share a huge chunk of my record certificate.

Major overseas players: John (Chicago), Carrie (Boston), Joost and Van der Valk Hotels (Holland), My in- laws Gabi, Marcela & Borek (Prague), Lado (Georgia), Akshay (India), John and Laurie (Thailand), Alan (Singapore/Thailand), Frank & Sandy (Perth) and Karen (Brisbane)

Warm Showers hosts: You all played a part, without Warm Showers, I would never have attempted the ride. Thank you Brian (Abbotsford, BC), Louis Marc (Revelstoke, BC), Sheila (Canmore, Alberta), Keri (Moose Jaw, Saskatchewan), Leon (Kola, Manitoba), Glen & Darby (Thief River Falls, Minnesota), Susan and Audrey (Brainerd, Minnesota), Nick (Luck, Wisconsin), Colton

(Galesville, Wisconsin), Alan and Alicia (Madison, Wisconsin), Jeremy (Mentor, Ohio), Vincent (Buffalo, NY), Stevie (Syracuse, NY), Jim (Albany, NY), Eszter & Paulo (Redondo, Portugal), Paco & Medina Del Campo Triathlon Club (Medina Del Campo, Spain), Luis & Maria (Burgos, Spain), Marina (Irun, Spain), Lydie & Pascal (Bordeaux, France), Davide & family (Nancy, France), Lina & Cord (Bremen, Germany), Donát & Mr Szalay, (Hungary) Gurol & Friends (Gelibolu, Turkey) Nurullah & friends (Trabzon, Turkey) Heather & Simon (Wilmington, Australia), Michael and Ellie (Dartmoor, Australia), Howard and Dianne (Shepparton, Australia), Hayden and family (Moree, Australia)

Other hosts and sponsored accommodation: Arno (Calgary Alberta), Bob and Cynthia (Medicine Hat, Alberta), David, family and friends (Toledo), Michael (Hartford), Sandra, (La Rochelle, France), Miros & Martine (Nante, France), Gitta (Vaals, Holland), Christoph (Halle Saale, Germany), Lenka (Brno, Czech Republic), Judith (Aubury, Australia), Eunice (Invercargill), Ken (Queenstown), Jackie and Craig (Orari), Greg and Bev (Spotswood), Peter & Anne (Taupo). Also Nina (Port Campbell Hostel, Australia), Millmerran Holiday Park, Australia & Levin Travelodge.

Family, friends and contributors to personal funding: Tony, Mike, Matt, Anne (Belgium), James (Dunedin), Dave (Tauranga), Nina & Dave (Tauranga), Sharon (Dunedin), Mike (Queensland),

Willy (Holland), my Dad and other family members.

Not forgetting bike helpers and other sponsored help: Greg, Steve and Stu at Avanti Plus Dunedin. John Winke (Keywin Sports), Yo, Mong Cycles (Chiang Mai), Alan, Graham & Steve (Invercargill), Sounds Air, Salmon World Cafe, Trevor (Avanti Plus Shepparton), Avanti Plus Perth, Map World (Christchurch), Tony (Watercooled Sports) and Tedde de Boer (Follow my Challenge).

To those who rode with me, tried to find help, gave advice or simply sent messages of support: Bryan (Timaru), Amol (Auckland), Hauraki Ice Racing Club, Rita (Christchurch), Nick (Blenheim), Chris (Moana Pool Gym), The Bentleys (Alberta), Parry, Bryony and Anita (CTCR), Steve, Tracy and Lily (Dunedin), Robert (Nelson), Lee (UK), Juliana (Italy), Tony & Janos (Dunedin).

Finally anyone else who, bought me a pie, met me on arrival in Dunedin or Auckland, commented or even liked my Facebook page and of course all those that contributed with CTCR donations.

Author's Note

Trying to categorise my story has been difficult. Potential hashtags could include Olympics, travel, adventure, cycling. But my story also touches on interesting philosophical questions about what it means to 'really live'. I would like to think hashtags such as motivation or inspiration are also appropriate. Given my diverse sports career, my work as a fitness instructor and my years around high performance athletes, I had hoped this book would also serve as a guide to exercise, health and sports performance. Sadly, there has not been scope to include many of my anecdotes and observations from these fields. I have however compiled sufficient left over content for a second book on exercise physiology and exercise psychology. The two can be hard to separate. Perhaps...*'Gymnasium Philosophy'- Who Makes it, Who Doesn't.*

Conscious that the New Zealand public cannot relate to the sport of speed skating I have reluctantly reduced much of the draft relating to my Olympic experiences. I also flagged the idea of getting the book on the shelves in New Zealand via the standard processes. But thanks to the increasingly popular concept of eBooks I have been able to bypass this process and tell my story.

It has taken me over a year and countless hours to finish this book. It required discipline and perseverance and like my self-coached Olympic career and world ride, I simply did it myself. Although those who have helped make this journey possible are acknowledged at the beginning, I certainly feel a great deal of personal ownership of this book and of my achievements. I am also proud that there has been no need for exaggeration, embellishment or the need for extreme use of artistic licence. What you read is what happened.

Introduction

'Breakdown'

"It ain't about how hard you hit. It's about how hard you can get hit and keep moving forward."

Rocky Balboa

October 16, 2015 DAY 67, GEORGIA:
Samtredia - Gori 230 km

The humpbacked receptionist now lay snoring face down on her desk in the dilapidated one star hotel. The previous night she had mimed that I should watch my back, bike and belongings carefully. She had warned me about venturing back out onto the streets where I had hoped to find proper food. "Bad mans" she had said, shaking her finger. I had taken her advice and locked myself in my room with some manky bread, vodka and a can of what I think was gizzard goulash. Needing to consume 7000 calories a day, I had little choice.

At 5:20 am I assumed that the mafia would have fallen asleep. I left my key on the desk and wheeled my bike quietly passed the helpful hump lady and out onto the grim streets of Samtredia. With no chance of a hot coffee, I clipped into my pedals and had breakfast on the run. It consisted of two caffeine tablets and the last of the bread, coated with some sort of Russian Nutella substitute. The first few kilometres were promising. I cycled on a traffic free section of brand new highway, but it soon diverted back to the old potholed road that ran parallel. The remainder of the highway's completion was scheduled for 2017. Bugger!

The last 67 days had taken me through nearly 16,000 km and 19 countries. I had averaged 220 km a day but I had fallen behind the world record due to a series of crises, the latest being floods along the Black Sea Coast in Eastern Turkey. A cold headwind picked up and I was riding slower than usual.

Above the increasing headwind I began to hear occasional clicking noises coming from my bottom bracket. A high pitched squeal suddenly vibrated through the carbon fibre frame. Tension increased in the pedal stroke, before it loosened completely and then jolted. The bearings in the bottom bracket were done! What would normally have been a smooth pedalling action was now interrupted by a shuddering THUNK with each pedal revolution. Eventually it would become metal on metal. Then metal on the carbon frame. It might get me to the capital Tbilisi, but then what? I had seen two bikes since I entered Georgia, both were vintage single speed Soviet relics, ridden by poor farmers.

I was prepared for the typical mechanical issues that would and had inevitably arisen throughout the journey. I carried the tools required to fix my chain, and those needed to replace spokes and cables. I also carried the necessary kit to fix punctures, of which I had had more than my share. The last had occurred in a downpour in Eastern Turkey two days earlier. I had lost my temper outside a gas station in typical style. In an enraged fit I had hurled the wheel into a bush, much to the amusement of my Turkish audience. But this collapsed bottom bracket was a problem I could not fix alone.

Throwing tantrums seemed to help me vent my frustration in minor bike issues but this was a biggie! I needed to stay calm. This was a critical moment in the race, I needed to recognise and control the situation.

The part had only served a quarter of its recommended shelf life and should have been reliable enough to get me right around the planet. But I had not expected it to be immersed in gritty Turkish rain for five straight days. Not even modern sealed bearing systems could have been expected to repel the road grime resulting from the endless downpours I had recently endured. The unexpected drowning of this essential part had clearly caused its early destruction.

I started up a mountain. The lack of decent food and the shuddering pedal stroke made for painfully slow progress over the 1,200 m Rikoti Pass that separates the green valleys of Western Georgia from the more barren and mountainous East. The axel was still holding the cranks to the frame, but the gradient became increasingly steeper. For the first time on the trip I considered pushing. Everything was tired by this point, my legs and lungs burned up the climb and my neck ached. I was going slow; but I was moving forward.

PTHISSSSSssssss! Thud thud thud thud thud... A new layer of noise from the rear wheel joined the jolting rhythm of the bottom bracket. Puncture number 34.

The tantrums and fits of rage that usually followed punctures sounded like a most excellent Iron Maiden song, but the puncture was the last of my worries. Besides, the energy required for a quality tantrum was gone. I had a bigger problem to deal with. My approach to the tube change was methodical and uncharacteristically calm. Twenty minutes later I resumed jolting along at no more than jogging speed over the mountain pass. By late afternoon I had descended and joined the old

Khashuri-Tbilisi highway.

A mixture of solid old Ladas and late model sedans played chicken on this busy but narrow highway of doom. Safety, seat belts and rules were clearly just for pedantic folk. Since descending the mountain I had opted to ride on the highway's gravel shoulder in favour of certain death. I wouldn't make Tbilisi tonight but I *was* closer to Tbilisi than I was one hour ago, and still moving forward.

I hit an upsized pothole, a loud and familiar crack shook through the frame. My seat collapsed from under me. The size of the pothole combined with the weight of my bag had proved too much for the last of my spare seat post bolts. Again I didn't bother with a tantrum, I needed to get moving again. I sheltered behind some trees while pondering a solution. I eventually solved this latest mechanical stress by cramming a tree branch into the tapered seat tube which stopped the seat from slipping. I scooped out the last of the Russian Nutella substance with my fingers and continued into the increasing headwind, which at least drowned out the irritating noise of my bike.

I don't ride with music. Cycling with headphones not only deprives you of the aural travel experience, but it's also dangerous. I needed to hear every one of the screaming horns and engines to remind me to keep my place in the gutter. Without a real playlist, I usually tried to fill my head with the most inspirational soundtracks of my life. Showing my age, Led Zeppelin and Pink Floyd were common, on an angry day perhaps Metallica. At around 5 pm and after nearly 12 hours of grovelling, my pace slowed further and the *thunking* of the cranks created a slower but steady beat. Jim Morrison's 'The End' entered my head... "This is the end...my only friend the end". Was this latest roadblock the end of the record? I'd done my best, I had some good stories already, but I was resigning to the probability that record was almost certainly over. Giving up, however, was out of the question. I wouldn't quit, I hadn't given up, I was just facing reality.

If my bike held out I would now arrive in Tbilisi on a Sunday night, with just a few hours to spare in Georgia before my non-changeable transfer flight over Afghanistan and Pakistan early on Monday. (For obvious reasons, Guinness rules permit a flight over this section as long as the kilometres were made up elsewhere). In this desolate former Soviet country, I would need to find specialised tools and a highly specialised part in less than 24 hours. I also still needed to cover the final 120 km to Tbilisi on a bicycle that was slowly dying. Get phone reception, try to get help. It was all I could do.

At the end of this long and troublesome day I would finally find cell phone coverage in the aptly named city of Gori. The standard distance of 230 km had been met but it had taken a miserable 14 hours. I rolled into this depressing and spooky town desperately looking for food and a place to sleep. I found something that looked like Pizza, but wasn't, before trying to find a bed for the night.

Georgian Roads

Gori had the same permanent, unfinished and abandoned look that is typical in Bulgaria. On the exact same streets, a boy named 'Ioseb Besarionis dze Jughashvili' was born in 1878.[1] Better known as Joseph Stalin, Stalin's cruelty could almost be forgiven, having been forced to grow up here. The town had a grim history and had been bombed by Russia as recently as the 2008 South Odessa war. I found a dreary hotel within my price range and fortunately some cell phone coverage! A call for help could finally be made. I was spent!

A glum looking Babushka slapped down a key after I handed over my 40 Lari. I reached for my phone and crashed on a hard mattress in a gloomy room. I had ferociously tried to mime the need for a Wi-Fi code or internet but a text would have to do. I closed the door and sent out a plea for help.

The going had got tough, tougher than most of the last 67 days, but I had controlled the controllable. I had adopted this key mantra during my Olympic skating years and it had got me through the day.

In his 2008 book *Our Olympic Century,* sports writer Joseph Romanos dubbed my/our very unknown story 'The New Zealand Speed Skating Phenomenon'. The book had dedicated two whole pages to a story that was indeed 'phenomenal'. In fact, it would have to go down as the greatest Winter Olympic underdog story of all time. The Jamaican bobsled team and 'Eddie the Eagle' were good, even made into award winning movies. But they had nothing on the New Zealand speed skating phenomenon.

Like Eddie and the Jamaicans, we (the New Zealand speed skating team) also had to overcome logistical and financial challenges just to qualify for the Olympics, but when we did, we nearly won a medal! We got 4th! The paper medal. There were two ice rinks in New Zealand at the time, no funding and no real coaching. In a pure, competitive and demanding Olympic sport, we made it to the very top. We broke world records; our relay team even became world champions.

I had taken on this world circumnavigation record in the same underdog fashion. Other than my bike there was no real sponsorship and little support. Without the experiences I had as a speed skater there was no way I would have made it this far on my trip or even got to the start line. The ability to tolerate discomfort, the physical conditioning and mental skills honed over three Olympic games had served me well on Day 67. But given the disastrous mechanical failure, the world record looked unlikely.

The fastest circumnavigation by bicycle is arguably the toughest endurance challenge imaginable. The record has only ever been attempted by a handful of mad men and two mad women since the first recording in 1984. The entry is free, but this is a completely un-marshalled event. Once your entry is accepted you don't even get a t-shirt, no course map, or even a sponsored energy bar, nothing! The record is difficult for Guinness officials to police and has been subject to several rule changes and controversial attempts. There is no distinction between supported and unsupported records. Most recent attempts have been supported. For the majority of my journey I would have no such luxury.

There have been several improvements on this rarely attempted challenge. Nick Sanders set an original record in 1984. On 13 February 2005, Steve Strange completed the first record attempt under the new Guinness rules, achieving a world record of 276 days and 19 hours. A well-documented record was completed in 2008, when Mark Beaumont completed a circumnavigation of the globe in 194 days and 17 hours. Beaumont's record was again beaten in 2010. Vin Cox completed a circumnavigation of the globe, which was certified by Guinness as the new World Record with a time of 163 days, 6 hours, 58 minutes.

This record was short-lived when Alan Bate completed a well-supported circumnavigation in 125 days 21 hours and 45 minutes, ratified by Guinness World Records. This record has also since been beaten unofficially by a couple of tough Englishmen. On 13 June 2014, Lee Fancourt completed a circumnavigation in a little more than 100 days, but sadly for Lee he was disqualified after failing to return to the point in India where he took a taxi in order to help out his support crew. Another English rider, Mike Hall, completed the record in 107 days. Again, this record was not ratified. Alan Bate's record of 125 days was the official benchmark.

The current women's record is 144 days by Paola Gianotti who started and finished at Ivrea, Turin, Italy, from 8 March to 30 November 2014. Her ride was fully supported. During her voyage, Paola was injured in a road accident which resulted in a fractured vertebra. Although the Guinness

World Record rules state that the clock does not stop, Paola's time was frozen for four months until she recovered and resumed her attempt on 18 September 2014. While it's legitimacy is therefore much debated, this is currently the official female record.

The previous women's record was held by Juliana Buhring of British/German nationality (though born in Greece). Juliana completed the circumnavigation in 152 days, becoming the first woman to attempt and to complete a circumnavigation of the world by bicycle, using a route that complies with the requirements of Guinness World Records. She was mostly unsupported.

The new rules state that the clock no longer stops for any waiting time, nor for transit flights or ferries. The clock is only stopped when the rider crosses the finish line after completing the circumnavigation. The journey must be continuous and in one direction (East to West, or West to East). The minimum distance ridden should be 18,000 miles (29,000 km). Among many other rules, these are stated: 'Any considerable distance travelled opposite to the direction of the attempt will be discounted from any calculations of the overall distance travelled' also 'The participant must pass through two approximate antipodal points during the attempt' and 'The entire journey must be tracked by the use of an accurate, professional equipment, GPS tracking device carried by the challenger, .kml files must be sent in as part of the evidence required.' [2]

In April 2015 I hadn't even considered the idea of breaking the world circumnavigation record. Four months later, I departed. How could someone possibly be prepared to take on a challenge of this scale with almost no funding or time for preparation? Surely it would take a life time of preparation. It would require a diverse skill set and personality type. I asked myself what was involved. Did I have the physical ability? Did I have the mental ability? Did I have the money?

I was 44, no spring chicken, but despite my age it was obvious that I still had the physical requirements. I ticked every box. A few months earlier I'd broken the New Zealand 24 hour cycling record. It wasn't long since I'd competed at the top end of the Coast to Coast Multisport race. If I had lost any youthful speed it wasn't showing, and besides this was not going to be a race about speed, it was going to be about slow and steady. In recent years, I'd been a competitive powerlifter. My muscles and joints were still strong and flexible. Whether I could ride over 230 km every day for four months straight was always going to be unknown, but if anybody was used to a daily beating, it was me.

I considered the mental and emotional requirements. Of course, I'd miss my wife but I was comfortable with my own time. I had demonstrated extreme examples of lonely perseverance over a lengthy and diverse sporting carrier. You needed nerves of steel to compete in speed skating, as you would riding through Indian cities. I'd competed in the Olympic Games, in a pressure sport where there was nowhere to hide. I'd worked closely with a professional sports psychologist. Through speed skating I had built excellent time management and other logistical skills, I'd been a fitness instructor, I understood nutrition. I'd been a bike mechanic, and had ridden in third world countries before. I'd even ridden part of the route before. I loved and understood geography, I had language skills and most importantly, I enjoyed seeing the world by bike. When I broke it down, I was made for the job. What about money?

Because of my dire employment situation, I was broke. An expedition around the world doesn't come cheap, but I was used to achieving big goals on small budgets. My Olympic skating career was proof of that. Besides, sitting around waiting for work was becoming seriously depressing. I'd find the money.

Chapter 1

'Tants'

"We used to say that he who threw the biggest tantrum won the day".
Neil Finn

I spent the first 16 years of my life in the same house, five kilometres from where I was born in central Auckland. I was the youngest of five siblings, with three brothers and a sister. A typical house in New Zealand's largest city. The city of sails, a pretty lucky place to start life.

Thanks to my siblings I ended up with the nickname 'Tants', short for Tantrums. When I went into a rage, I did it properly. My tantrums become legendary for their ferocity and intensity. If I was going to fight, I'd fight my hardest. The legend grew that it took six grown men and the help of the local fire department to change my nappy. I put in a solid effort whatever the odds.

By 10 years of age I was no less stubborn. My parents were proud of how I always got good 'effort marks' in my school reports, but I understood what my school report meant. I wanted achievement marks! I wasn't happy with all this 'at least you tried' crap. I was always going to try, but I wanted to do well! I was highly competitive, but only averagely talented.

One lunch time, the sporty kids were bragging about who was the fastest runner in the class. Their arguments were going nowhere so they turned to discuss who was the slowest. I cringed, knowing my name would probably come up. The committee agreed that either I or Gregory Gibson, the choir enthusiast, were likely contenders and somehow goaded us into a race. After a poor start I beat Gibson. I wasn't a natural athlete and nearly always the smallest kid in the class, but I would not be the slowest Room 1 kid in the 1980 May Road Primary 30 metres. No way!

I would fight to be right, and throw massive tantrums in brotherly cricket tournaments. Being the youngest by three years *and* a sore loser inevitably meant trouble in the back yard. Games would either end my way, by lost ball or in tears. I would try my hardest to win the game and fight to get my way. Windows were often broken and blood was often shed on the Richardson Road Oval.

Controversial LBW decisions would be the main cause of violence. I would stand my ground and refuse to leave the crease when given out. A solid spanking was never enough to deter me from arguing with my brothers who assumed the role of both umpire and ground security. I would just keep fighting back until I couldn't. I would have to be incapacitated to be removed. It was like a scene from the apocalyptic Zombie movies. I just kept on coming, whatever injuries had been inflicted.

Having separated, my parents were never around to mediate and the neighbours were probably too terrified to intervene with the devil child from next door. My tantrums made John McEnroe's seem as calm as the Dalai Lama. The name 'Tants' or sometimes Tanty had become justifiably well established.

A sense of adventure, a passion for travel and having the ability to push through discomfort were essential traits required for my world ride. Fortunately, my family set some excellent examples. My Mum and Dad spent their life savings to emigrate with the whole family to New Zealand in 1968. Working in the stressful commercial art business in London, Dad put everything on the line and the whole family on a boat, and set out to a fabled paradise in the South Pacific. They found New Zealand and he immediately instilled in us a sense of appreciation for the country. We knew we were growing up in a lucky land. Every weekend Dad would remind us and take us on long tramps in Auckland's Waitakere Ranges and along West Coast beaches. I usually enjoyed it, but being the youngest it wasn't always easy to keep up. Occasionally I would stop for a tantrum, but nobody was coming back to carry me. The walks also served as early lessons in pushing through discomfort.

"The race is won by the rider who can suffer the most"
Eddy Merckx

My brother Chris first showed me what suffering looked like on Christmas Eve 1978. Chris could push himself! He could tolerate discomfort, pain and set about challenges with a mathematical and systematic approach. He was the last kid to get in any sort of fight at school, but boy, could he fight a bicycle. At the family Christmas gathering my poor old auntie had been given an exercise bike to help with her circulation. The Nicholson kids and our numerous cousins gathered around the bike, unable to resist the temptation to play on the shiny new contraption. But like most exercise machines, the bike looked like a lot more fun than it was.

Chris must have been about 11 and politely waited for his turn. He had been busy doing the calculations to work out how long it might take him to ride 10 km, about 9.5 km further than anyone else to that point. Everyone assumed he would soon give up the frantic pace at which he set out but within a couple of minutes, he settled into a rhythm. He was bright red, breathing deeply, dripping with sweat and fully focused on the dial.

Chris had no intention of slowing down, let alone stopping. Chris was one of those rare kids who enjoyed school cross country. He set goals, did the maths and worked out what he needed to do to get there. He could take the pain.

Chris Nicholson became twice New Zealand Cycling Champion and represented his country in two sports, at three Olympic Games. He became a world champion speed skater and the only male Olympian to represent New Zealand at both the Summer and Winter Olympics. Like my other siblings Chris was an inspiration.

I'd been exposed to some impressive tales of adventure and travel already. My sister Sara had recently returned from surfing with sharks and crocodiles in Indonesia.

My oldest brother Paul was 17 at the time. He has missed the Christmas gathering. He had been busy working and saving for what would be the first of many intrepid Asian adventures.

Paul was sick of everyone making a fuss about Chris's measly 10 km. Who cares how fast you go; how far can you go? Paul asked. On Boxing Day he boldly declared he would ride his steel framed three speed the 190 km from Auckland to Whitianga, a quiet holiday destination where we would spend our summer caravan holiday. The family laughed, Paul usually never rode further than the local tennis club and nobody took him seriously. Determined to prove us wrong Paul left before sunrise. We caught up with him around midday as he grumpily cycled into headwinds on the Hauraki Plains. His denim stubbies had already caused some serious chaffing.

Refusing a lift and already exhausted, Paul insisted on plodding on alone in the summer heat over the hilly, gravel roads of the Coromandel Ranges. We drove ahead to the campground, spending the afternoon playing on the beach and setting up camp. I had a tantrum. I'd lost a game of something.

As darkness approached, my Dad assumed Paul had been defeated. He would have to backtrack to wherever he find Paul, hopefully still alive. But Paul didn't need to be rescued. Just then, covered in dust, dehydrated and suffering heatstroke Paul wobbled into the camp. He had done it. He actually cycled to Whitianga, in a day! I was impressed. He had established the first official family 'grovel ride' record. In my eyes, it was a world record. 190 km in horrid conditions. Paul had set a benchmark that would inspire a family of bike grovelers.

In terms of distance, Paul's ride was considered mediocre by the standards Chris and I would later set as Olympians and Multisport athletes. But by then we were trained athletes on carbon fibre racing bikes. Our suffering was nothing compared to what Paul had endured in the inaugural record.

We formed the Nicholson Grovel-Ride Federation (NGF) to moderate our claims to the title. We eventually decided that daily distance alone should not define the record. 'Manly points' could be added for hardships. Paul had certainly experienced plenty of hardships.

In the days before molly coddling, my Dad encouraged adventure. On family holidays near Opotiki, Dad would drop us 30 km up the Waioeka Gorge in a basic 2-man canoe. The idea was that we would survive the rapids and reappear later that day, through the surf, at our camp on the beach. Somehow we always did, usually washed up, and capsizing in the surf. It was scary at times, but great fun!

30 years later I would paddle down the same river as an experienced kayaker in part of the Motu Challenge multisport race. There was a strict safety briefing for the athletes. The river has Grade 2 rapids and competitors are expected to have Grade 2 experience. What my Dad did would be described by many as irresponsible, but as a kid, the reward of great days' adventure was well worth the risk. He made us wear life jackets and the first time I landed on the beach felt like I had been on the Lewis and Clark expedition.

In the August holidays of 1981 I went ice

skating for the first time, at the newly built Paradice Ice Arena in Avondale. I had attended a few boogie sessions during the disco craze at the local roller skating rink and I wanted to try ice skating. My brother Richard had also been hanging out at the ice rink discos. Chris was allowed to try ice skating for the first time with his older brother at a late-night session. I wasn't allowed to go and threw a tantrum.

In the final five minutes of the session Chris had fallen and spilt his head open. His head needed to be heavily stitched, but he glossed over the fall as if it was nothing. Chris didn't mind pain, he couldn't wait to go back. As soon as his stitches were removed I eagerly followed him along to the ice skating rink for my first time. I fell in love with it instantly!

I felt confident at the ice rink. I was clumsy in most sports but I got the hang of ice skating quickly. I wasn't disadvantaged by my size and I looked forward to each public session, arriving early in anticipation. I would rather race around fast than learn fancy tricks. The music, lights and disco atmosphere at the rink were an added attraction. I'd speed around trying to impress girls, taking the occasional break off the ice, and spending any left-over 20c on Frogger, Donkey Kong and other games. The latest '80s hits were pumping out on the speakers. I was on a Pac Man high score, Olivia Newton John's 'Let's get physical' played in the background while I became cornered trying to get to the banana. I smacked the screen, had a tantrum and headed back to the ice.

Soon I was attending as many public sessions as my pocket money would afford. I got my first pair of ice hockey skates for Christmas, way better than the rentals. A few months later we were approached by members of Auckland's Hauraki Ice Racing Club who were looking at establishing the club at the new rink. They'd seen Chris and I tearing around dangerously and racing through the wobbly public. We were constantly being sent off for speeding by the rink stewards. We hadn't thought about ice skating as a sport. We were told figure skating was gay and ice hockey had yet to be established. Speed skating was more our style anyway.

The speed skating club had been in existence since 1972 at the horribly undersized Glen Innes Rink on the other side of Auckland. A tall, quietly spoken and future Olympian named Matthew Biggs was the leader of the speed group, he encouraged Chris and I to attend the first speed skating sessions. I blew all my savings on my first pair of speed skates, Bauer Planets. A shocking design by today's standards but I didn't know any difference, to me they were unbelievably special. It was like having daggers on your feet! Once you got used to them speed skates were fast but hard to control! Eventually speed skates were banned in public sessions, Chris and I had caused one too many accidents.

1983 Andrew Nicholson at Paradice Ice Rink, Auckland In the days before helmets and barrier safety pads

Chris joined Matthew Biggs and a few of the club's older skaters at the 1982 New Zealand Championships in Invercargill. My dad reluctantly allowed 15 year old Chris to blow all his paper-run money on the train fare. There was no real coach, just a bunch of youngsters off on an adventure to the other end of the country.

Chris returned from Invercargill, having placed second overall in the juniors. I was massively proud and lapped up his exciting tales from the National Championships. In New Zealand the sport was tiny but compared to our club sessions in Auckland, Chris made it seem huge. His story differed from the travel tales told by my older siblings, but it was no less inspiring. Chris was engrossed in the racing. There was more to ice skating then just the local rink. It was real sport, it was even in the Winter Olympics!

A year later I took my own first skating trip to the New Zealand outdoor champs, which were to be held on natural ice on a flooded Twizel quarry. We drove down from Christchurch, but sadly a warm wind blew up before the competition and turned the skating track into a swimming pool. The officials announced the cancellation, I threw a tantrum, and cried all the way back to Christchurch.

The Auckland kids now had to kill three days waiting for our return flight. Our host, the New Zealand Champion Mark Atkinson, had a variety of inspirational skating magazines and video tapes lying around his home. Having never seen skating on TV we spent hours going through the tapes, gaining an appreciation of the scale of the sport in Northern Europe and other countries. The packed European stadiums and crowds cheering competitors through snow storms on the big 400 m tracks made a huge impression. These guys were tough! Mark also had tapes from the 1980 Winter Olympics. I watched American skater and later pro cyclist Eric Heiden dominate each event. I had found a sports hero I could relate to. Until this point I had wanted to be the All Black Gary Knight. I thought he was tough after watching him get hit by the flour bomb in the controversial South African '81 Springbok tour.

Like most kiwi kids, I had been exposed to rugby culture, you couldn't help it. My dad and brother Richard were big fans. I enjoyed watching the All Black games and when I was eight I promised myself I would become an All Black. Naturally I was inspired by who our country told us we should admire as sports heroes.

But I wasn't passionate about the game and way too young to have any idea of what becoming an All Black would have meant. Firstly, I didn't even belong to a club, we played one on one rugby in the back yard where the fights were as frequent as they were in cricket matches. My brother Richard had to play on his knees to make it fair. I was too small to play at school and got pushed out to the wing. On the rare occasion the ball came my way I would usually panic and drop it.

Returning from Christchurch, there was no parent waiting for me at the airport. I was dropped off at home, with school tomorrow, Dad was away somewhere. Since my parents had split up the house was a bombsite. Richard was 18 now, a serious party had taken place. My bedroom stank, I went randomly between Mum and Dad's place at the time. Paul was smuggling Bibles into China and Sara was living in the Himalayas. My family was breaking up, growing up and going in all sorts of directions.

The next morning Chris woke me up late for school. The milk was solid in the bottle so I found some bread for breakfast. Dad had at least left us some lunch money. I grumpily trod off to school. After my skating trip it was a morning of gloom and a big anti-climax. Monday morning reality had also interrupted a fantastic and vivid dream. 20 minutes earlier I had been racing in a major long track skating event. It had been snowing.

Walking home that day, I thought about my dream, and promised myself I would become an Olympic speed skater. I would follow this dream. A switch went on - 'It's a big goal, a big promise, I'd better try my hardest?' I thought about what it meant to try one's hardest? I assumed it meant doing more and pushing harder than everyone else.

Smack! Hit from behind I went down hard, the contents of my duffle bag spread across the sidewalk. I'd been clotheslined by the local BMX bully, Dean. Pens, and a mouldy sandwich that had been there since Mum left, spread across the road. Dean was the prop for Mt Roskill Intermediate First 15. There was no reason for the clothesline, Dean just did it for kicks. "Fucking dick" I yelled, he spun around. "What u call me?" I told him again and was soundly beaten, but often I held my own in school fights. Going ballistic helped and compensated for my small stature. I'd also had had plenty of practice trying to take on big brothers. On this occasion going ballistic wasn't enough. Dean left me with some head bruising and rode off.

I was angry. I had fewer friends at school since I'd started skating. They did normal kiwi things, rugby, like Dean. I wiped away the blood and tears and went back to thinking about my promise, now more determined than ever to make it mean something. I knew that I hadn't kept my All Black promise, but I didn't even like the game anymore. I loved skating. I would keep this promise. Training would start today. I wouldn't just 'go ice skating' anymore; I would train, like an athlete. I would do my best.

Gary Knight's rugby poster was the last to come down. I replaced him with a crumpled picture of Eric Heiden that I had pinched from a magazine at Mark Atkinson's house. I was 12 now, I had a clearer idea of what 'trying hard' meant. I found the stopwatch and walked to the front gate.

Chapter 2

Promises

"Promises are like crying babies in a theatre, they should be carried out at once."
Norman Vincent Peale

From now on I'd run a daily a time trial; from the gate to the phone box down the road, and back. Running had to be better than nothing. Apart from public sessions I only got to skate at the club twice a week. I knew I could do more. If I could beat my time, I correctly figured I was getting fitter, and that had to be good for skating.

If I couldn't go skating, I'd do my run, then hops, jumps and imitation exercises till I could barely walk. I figured if I could do one more jump than the previous day, I had to be improving? I also figured correctly that elsewhere in the world, kids my age were skating every day with quality coaches and equipment. I would just have to try and train another way. Eric Heiden had shown how skating helped cycling so Chris and I correctly figured the opposite had to be true. If I could get myself a racing bike there would be no stopping me.

Chris had already acquired a ten speed and had started going on cycling tours with Paul during the summer holidays. They travelled around Northland and East Cape, and came back with exciting stories of exploration and suffering. Chris had also been starting to race. He claimed a new NGF family distance record, aged only 16, riding 220 km from Tauranga to Auckland into a headwind, plus manly points.

I wanted to go riding with Chris but there was no way I could keep up with him on the Chopper I used for my paper run. Besides, it had been out of action since a jump gone wrong at the BMX track. Dean had thoroughly enjoyed watching me loose skin then wheel away the mangled wreck of a bike that was never designed for stunts.

My Dad either couldn't or wouldn't help me, but within a few months I had saved enough on my own to buy a second hand, oversized Raleigh Arena ten speed. I called it a racing bike. It had alloy wheels and toe clips. I also took off the mudguards, stand and carrier. I made it as fast as I could, but in reality, it was just a slightly souped-up ten-speed.

Chris had already crashed his ten speed and bought a Healing Shogun, and I joined him at races. My first events were the Saturday morning 16 km Auckland waterfront time trials. Like my run to the letter box, I set about slowly improving. As well as racing, I'd try to follow Chris on adventurous long rides. My bike had given me the freedom to explore and the ride to Piha Beach was a regular test. Chris would go out and ride the brutally steep hill several times. He was miles better than me, even if I rode in his slipstream I'd struggle to keep up. If I wanted to join him on a long ride he made clear that it was a 'no mercy ride'. "If you can't keep up, too bad" and he would abandon me. Chris was getting good, he couldn't wait for me! He had made a promise himself, he was already New Zealand's best junior skater and wanted to go to the world skating champs. He quit school, saved every cent from his job at the furniture shop and went to the 1985 world champs in Amsterdam aged 17. On his first attempt, he placed 21st. A skinny, blonde kid from New Zealand showed up without a coach and in the longer races he managed to tear the legs off some world class skaters.

My first logical step to making it to the Olympics was to start competing beyond New Zealand. All skating trips had to be self-funded. The association had no money and my first trip to the Australian Champs was funded from my job after school, pumping gas at a BP in Mt Eden. My Dad had set the job up. He might not have handed me the easy cash but he helped me help myself. I could barely reach the pumps and on several occasions customers asked where the boss was.

Back from winning the Australian sub junior

champs, I was straight into training for the next year. I followed Chris's example, improved and by the time I was 16 I started to think about to getting myself to the World Champs. I continued to train as hard as possible, especially on the bike. I could never dream to own a bike like the other kids in the cycling club. Skates and airfares for skating trips were my priority. It was either turn up on an oversized bike with antique gear, or not race at all. I'd turn up on whatever I had. The fits of rage I threw in yard games were now happening on the road. With cheap second-hand gear, things were always breaking down. I ended up throwing tantrums (and often my bike) on rides, it was frustrating to constantly have to make do. The bicycle tantrum would be with me for years to come. Road rage took on a new meaning.

I set about trying to improve on time trials along the Auckland waterfront, stripping down my bike further by taking off the back brakes. I was determined to break 25 minutes. Maximising a tailwind, I was flying. A trucky was taking a turn inland and failed to spot the flying boy. Even with both brakes I would have made contact, with only one I had no chance. Truck, 1, skinny teenage 16 year old cyclist, nil.

My Dad was horrified when he arrived at the hospital, seeing the look of concern on the doctor's face while I lay semiconscious and moaning about back pains. My back was fine. My puncture repair kit and the kitchen forks serving as tyre levers in the back pocket of my bike jersey were digging into my back. I was devastated when my one and only woollen bike jersey had to be cut from my bruised body. A couple of weeks later I had recovered from severe concussion and a shoulder injury, I was back training, working and saving.

At my first World Championships in Montreal I was only 16 and would finish dead last but I was in no way discouraged. I knew I had time. I learned from the experience and the trip had given me the travel bug. On return I realised that I needed more time to make enough money to get to the next year's World Championships in St Louis, USA.

I was a total loner at school. I quit school and picked up a job in a sandwich bar in the city, before being offered a job working as a boat builder's labourer by a kind and gigantic Dutchman named Hank from our skating club. Hank would support me by offering me employment, with the essential two months off each year for the big trip. I was going to get to the top but it was obviously going to take time, sacrifice and training.

The dedication over the following years was extraordinary. On the mornings I had ice, I would rise at 5:15am, cycle to the rink and blow myself to pieces on the ice with brutal intervals, maximising every moment of precious ice time. I needed to be at work by 8:30am and I raced the hilly 30 km to Kumeu, where I would set to work grinding back welds, sweeping floors and being a general dog's body. I would then cycle the 30 km home each day. When ice time wasn't available I would either go to the gym after work, throw weights around, or train on a slide board, a poor and boring substitute for actual ice. Saturdays were usually dedicated to a bike race. At times my fanatical and extreme regime probably did more harm than good but I certainly became aerobically fit.

The absolute lack of coaching or support was, in many respects, a blessing. There was no one to force elaborate so called scientific programmes on us. The body somehow took the beatings and somehow adapted. I knew that what I was doing was working, because the stopwatch said so. I was going faster, both on the ice and on the bike. Everything was a time trial. It was about faster, longer, further or heavier, the basics. I developed an iron will, learned to take failure and tolerate a lot of discomfort. I built resilience.

By now Chris and I were among the best skaters in New Zealand, junior or senior. The association couldn't refuse putting our entries in for the World Champs. We weren't expecting money, our times weren't embarrassing, all they had to do was send in an entry. They let us go, we didn't even get a tracksuit and would turn up in rags. For the next four years I would work, train, save, beg, steal and borrow and very slowly improve. There was no financial support, no parental support. My proudest moments in my life were not winning world championships or breaking world records, but the perseverance and dedication I showed as teenager. Needless to say, when I see the sense of entitlement shown by today's generation of teenagers, I am often left shaking my head.

Chapter 3

1990 – The NZ Speed Skating Phenomenon

While Chris, Matthew and I were beginning to make our mark as skaters and step out into the international scene, Christchurch skaters Mike McMillen and Tony Smith had been pushing us hard at national championships. Mike McMillen had joined me at my second World Championships in the USA, where I improved and placed 32nd.

Skating came first for Mike, he was a motivated and dedicated athlete. Mike also had little support, he also worked hard, trained hard, and had to do things on the cheap.

My fourth World Champs were in Amsterdam, 1990, where Mike and I finally made a breakthrough. I got through the heats for the first time, placed 20th and was elated to be finally rewarded for my dedication. Mike won several major internationals. Small amounts of money filtered in. Matthew Biggs was now working and skating in England. He joined Chris, Mike and I for a budget tour of Europe and we put together a New Zealand relay team.

Relays in short track speed skating are 5000 m of bedlam. The race is 45 laps with teams of four skaters rotating on and off the track by means of a push. Precise timing of changes is essential, as is knowing your teammates. There is no set distance per skater; like a cycling madison, skaters can change at any point in the race. It generally comes down to seven turns of 15-20 seconds, each within around seven minutes. By the final rotations your legs start to fall off and most skaters begin to slow down. Unless, of course, you were a good cyclist. Chris was National Cycling Champion and the rest of us were fit. New Zealand suddenly had a relay team. It was fit, and it was flying.

The 1991 season was the qualifying year for the Albertville 1992 Winter Olympics. We were on form and with only five or six quality skaters to work with, selection soon became automatic and enabled us to focus as a unit. The national team made up for half the serious skaters in the country. But within a year we had beaten everyone! Even countries like Canada and Japan, who had thousands to choose from. Our relay team won the Pacific Rim Champs, and we were becoming confident. How was this possible? New Zealand suddenly had a world class speed skating team.

The one and only qualifying event for the Olympic Games was the 1991 World

Championships. Conveniently for us they were to be held in Sydney for the first and only time. There wouldn't even be a massive airfare to pay. We could afford more time to train. Qualifying was a ruthless and simple selection process. Make the semi-final (top 8) and were Olympians.

We drew a tough quarter final; USA, Italy and China. A few laps into the race Matthew tangled with a Chinese skater and crashed! Recovering from a crash at this level was unlikely but fitness was becoming a factor. The Olympic dream looked over, but we recovered, passed and beat the United States on the final lap. Remarkable. We went on to the final. We didn't just make it to the Olympics. We went in at number two!

New Zealand Short Track Speed Skating Team, 1992 Albertville Olympics. Matthew Biggs, Tony Smith, Mike McMillen, Chris Nicholson, Andrew Nicholson

Walking into the opening ceremony at my first Olympics was certainly a surreal moment. It was strange to finally get treated like an athlete. Trips were properly funded, for the first time. Olympic uniforms and small amounts of sponsorship were certainly valued after so many years of self-funding.

We even had support, Mark Atkinson became coach by default, but ultimately, we were a self-coached team. Nobody in New Zealand had ever acquired as much experience as the actual skaters. We were good and we had trained hard, but we were not yet a fully professional team. This would show in the Olympic Games where we went on to place a heart breaking 4th.

Although we had beaten Japan in the last three international races, they pipped us on the line in the final to take bronze. After the event, some team members argued that Tony Smith and Matthew Biggs should have been substituted after the semi-final to allow a fresh skater for the final. Tony Smith would eventually line up for both. He made a powerful start and gave it his absolute best but we faded in the final laps. Perhaps the support staff may have made a poor call, perhaps not, but the support staff were part of the team. We deserved 4th, end of story.

Moments after the event I was so convinced we were going to win a medal I stayed on the ice, somehow assuming I'd see the letters DQD (disqualified) on the scoreboard next to another nation. We were supposed to get a medal? What was happening? Apart from the celebrating Koreans I was the last to get off the ice, still staring at the scoreboard, willing for a change in result. 4th. Poor Mike McMillen also placed 4th in the individual 1000m.

After the dust settled it was time for a review of the team's performance and with the 1994 Lillehammer Olympics approaching, it was time to get things back on track. The decision not to substitute skaters in the Olympic final had caused rifts within the team, but grievances were soon resolved with a change in support staff.

We were assigned Mark Sutherland (coach of Kiwi gold kayaking medallists Ian Ferguson and Paul MacDonald) and performance coach/sports psychologist Craig Lewis. Both were to be highly influential in taking us to a new level of professionalism.

The team culture was polished, and our ability to focus on goal orientated processes was added to our already ingrained culture of hard work and self-discipline. For me, Craig's involvement was to begin a period of huge personal growth. Through Craig I developed mental skills that would contribute to both everyday life and future sports projects and especially to my world ride.

As always, training both on and off the ice was disciplined, hard and focused; but a sense of humour, friendship and ownership had become part of the team. We would make up silly songs about each other, play curling with drink bottles and other silly games between intervals, yet we never missed the go time.

An Olympic medal in the relay was the focus for the team, but I continued to improve as an individual skater. In a 1500m race at the Pacific Rim Championships in Japan I set out at an extraordinary pace, managing to tear the legs off the pure sprinters in my race, breaking and briefly holding the world record. I would never have dreamed that it was the first of three entries into the Guinness Book of World Records. I also made the top 8 in the 500m and placed 12th overall at the 1993 World Championships, but the best was yet to come. The disappointment of the 1992 Olympics was soon to be forgotten.

The 1993 World Championships in Beijing served as the qualifier for the 1994 Olympics. We had won our semi-final and by making the final were already assured of Olympic qualification.

For the moment, there was a World Championship title at stake. I looked at my teammates, knowing absolutely that each of them had done the best they could, to be the best they could be. Not just in recent months, but for over a decade. The World Championship final was underway.

After 3000m, the race had become a nail biter between the Italians and New Zealand, with USA and Australia struggling to hold contact. A poor change with nine laps to go left Italy with a 20-metre gap. The race would come down to who would slow down the least, the Italians had the advantage but were shutting down.

Taking more than my share of laps I was now making an impression on my opponent, fitness was becoming a factor. On his last exchange, my brother Chris closed the gap further, and then Mike McMillen cut down the remainder with a spectacular pass on the final lap. New Zealand were World Champions! We had also broken the world record by four seconds, I would make a second entry into the Guinness Book of World Records.

We deserved the win which extended to the support staff. Thanks to them we had become a team ahead of our time. We took a Weet-Bix box up to the Great Wall of China to show support for Sanitarium, who were a minor sponsor. Just like Gary Knight in 1978, I too would get on the Weet-Bix box.

Six months earlier Chris had ridden to an impressive 10th place at the Barcelona Olympics in the 100 km team time trial with cycling legends Graeme Miller, Brian Fowler and Paul Leitch. It was a credible ride with some tough team mates but

Chris confessed that the sense of connection was nowhere near the one that he felt to his speed skating team. Chris had grown up with the skating team. It rarely changed and each member had shared the same sacrifices, for over a decade. We became a tight family unit and shared a highly deserved and special moment.

It all came unstuck 10 months later at the Lillehammer Olympics, which proved to be a bridge too far. The relay team finished 8th and there was to be no individual success. Both Chris and Matthew Biggs had been dealing with injuries and without depth in New Zealand, quality replacement skaters simply didn't exist. Sadly, Lillehammer was the one and only time we had any significant media attention and we failed miserably. The team was not remembered as the champions they deserved to be. Lillehammer was to be a sad and final chapter to the speed skating phenomenon.

I was by far the youngest of the team and it was obvious that my team would disband after the Lillehammer Olympics. Chris and the others went home to be normal, they took up jobs and spent much neglected time with loved ones.

I would be left to compete as an individual skater. I would leave New Zealand and switch to the long track code of speed skating, where I would develop more traits and skills that would eventually contribute to my world ride. In 2000, after 18 years of trying, travel, highs and lows, I hung up my skates and returned to New Zealand. I had more or less fulfilled my child dream, but the necessity to put skating first had come at a cost. I was penniless and had little in the way of valuable work experience, qualifications or career prospects.

Chapter 4

Now What

2000: I had gained a qualification in fitness, having completed a fitness trainer's certificate in 1997. The course was woefully inadequate, unless you had been an Olympic athlete with a background in strength and fitness, which fortunately I had. On my return to New Zealand I picked up a job at a gym in Tauranga and eventually set up some personal training. Being around gym culture and away from ice rinks, I soon became interested in strength training. Skating had already made me strong, as well as fit.

I became involved in the sport of powerlifting, a pure test of strength. I wasn't a brilliant design for powerlifting, long gangly arms were a major disadvantage in the bench press, but I progressed with intense quality workouts and got competitive with a basic and systematic approach. I was never fully committed to powerlifting and still enjoyed cycling on the side, I'd occasionally race in major events and even at national championships but I wasn't fully committed to either sport which were at opposite ends of the strength and endurance spectrum. As far as powerlifting was concerned, I just kept putting weight on the bar; personal best, personal best. The fear of not getting a personal best became my motivator, just as it had with skating. In time, I competed in a couple of National Championships, once placing second in the 82.5 kg class. I eventually ended up with massive 240kg squat and deadlifts and a 130kg bench. Not bad for the smallest kid in the class. Powerlifting gave me something else to do while I figured out how I would spend the rest of my life.

I wasn't motivated to make it in personal training as a business or as a 'career'. I earned enough to survive and went on a couple of exotic and cheap cycling tours. Southern India, Vietnam. Recognized as a Nicholson Grovel Ride record I once rode a 210 km day, while touring India, with a bout of Delhi Belly. Lugging everything I needed for a 4 week tour I struggled over potholed roads, through blaring horns, pollution, heat and other hazards that cycling in India presents. I had no idea this trip would later serve as valuable experience for another epic challenge.

Money was just something to earn for cool experiences, I didn't want stuff. My clients were happy to pay me. Many of them were Tauranga real estate agents, motivated only by appearance. Having failed to exercise for 15 years, they were now expecting me to 'tone them up for summer'. Fitness and fat loss doesn't come so easy. I supplemented this with training a few top Bay of Plenty Rugby players but found the Rugby scene to be a culture of laziness and thuggery. Even with massive contracts within reach, the concept of training for these guys consisted of turning up to practice twice a week, the occasional footy run and some random bench press. I grew tired of gym culture, powerlifting and working with people less motivated than myself. I needed a new sport, and a 'proper' career.

After years of winters I also wanted to get outside more, enjoy the climate and nature of New Zealand. What a better way to enjoy it than multisport? Perhaps triathlon? My friend Warren from the cycling club convinced me to enter an event. My girlfriend tried to teach me to swim, like a swimmer. Until that point all I had done was the breaststroke and dog paddle that had somehow kept me afloat as a kid. It was a miracle I never drowned in family holidays, always taking risks trying to follow older and more competent brothers body surfing on West Coast beaches.

I was a trained Olympic athlete but I was a technical mess in the water. I entered an event at Mount Maunganui. It was a large field with a staggered start, the women starting five minutes behind the men. I was a man, apparently, but it was hard to tell if I was swimming or drowning. I emerged from the 1 km swim, only to find myself surrounded by large and elderly females who were all chatting together and waiting to ride the bike leg with their friends. Their goal was clearly 'to finish', and they had started five minutes behind me. No amount of cycling or running was going to make up for my swim. If you want to be a good swimmer, you start at age 3, not 33. Swimming has less to do with fitness and lots to do with technique. I was no swimmer. Besides, swimming was too slow for me.

I had a tiny bit of kayaking experience, thanks to my dad throwing me down dangerous rapids as a kid. A couple of weeks later I borrowed a boat and did the Kaimai Classic Multisport Race. I got 4th, and I was hooked!! A couple of months later I had a go at the Motu Challenge, down the river of death. I placed well and had a blast. I entered the 'Coast to Coast'.

2008 Coast to Coast, a well-deserved 'Speights'

This iconic race covers 243 km of cycling, mountain running and kayaking - it is held annually and the one day race is considered the World Championship of Multisport. As the name suggests the race goes from coast to coast, traversing the spectacular wilderness of New Zealand's South Island, from Kumara Beach near Greymouth to Sumner Beach in Christchurch. The 36 km mountain run crosses the main divide, up and down boulder strewn river beds. The 70 km kayak includes challenging white water rapids down the isolated Waimakariri river, the rest is by bicycle. Even the two-day race is not for the faint hearted.

Not mucking about, it was straight into the one-day race. My cycling was strong and my running average, but I soon realised that kayaking, like swimming, takes time and technique. I finished 30th in my first race, having fallen out of the kayak three times, as North Islanders who haven't had access to white water usually do. Again, strength and fitness can't match a skilled kayaker. I recorded the fastest final bike time, beating the winner Steve Gurney by seven minutes on the bike leg. Unfortunately, he had taken an hour out of me on the kayak, and nearly as much on the run.

I had a blast in my first race, it taught me a

great deal with regards to nutrition, organising equipment and increased my ability to tolerate long days of discomfort. I returned to Tauranga unable to bear the thought of selling my motivation to others at the gym. It really was time for a career. Society's 'shoulds' were putting me under pressure.

I took out a student loan and went to University to become a teacher, albeit 10 years later than the average Kiwi in my class. Given my enjoyable coaching experiences with kids, I thought I had much to offer.

At first I was confused as to why I seemed to be resented by most of my predominantly female peers. I was resented for getting good marks. I was resented for being fit and resented for putting assignments in on time. "Cs get degrees" was the class motto. Word soon got out at that I was an Olympian and I began to sense more bitterness and envy. I was resented because I had done; those who can, do; those who can't, teach. My classmates, it seemed, had chosen teaching by default. Tall poppy syndrome was alive and well in New Zealand.

My experience of university was a joke. A 9am - midday university lecture usually began at about 9:20. The 'classroom centred lecturer' looked on, nodding approvingly, as the training teachers were given the opportunity to express their feelings about the perceived struggles of university life. From 9.00 I would sit, tapping my pen and hoping to learn something. Perhaps something trivial, like teaching literacy. I'd give up at 9:10 and use my time wisely, by going over some notes. At 9:30 the lecture would actually start. We would hear all about the positive benefits of inquiry learning and child centred classrooms. The 15 minute break would commence at about 10:20 and finish about 11:00, just as soon as everyone was ready. About 11:40 everyone including the lecturer would agree that it had been a tough morning, it was time to wind up. Three hours of lectures had been turned into one. I stuck it out, did the work efficiently, kept professional and got through. The degree wasn't worth using as toilet paper, but as long as it got me a job.

I was living in Te Puke at the time, the kiwifruit capital of the world. I was done with gyms but still needed extra cash to support my student life. A buddy gave me holiday work at a kiwifruit orchard, where I was to meet my future wife Marcela, who I had also seen at the gym. We were pruning kiwifruit. I was now 34 years old, completely broke and saddled with a student loan.

Marcela was perfect, from the Czech Republic; on an extended working holiday and supporting her five year old Kiwi-born daughter, Patricia. I assumed Marcela was out of my league, but you don't know if you don't try.

She was fit. Back in the Czech Republic Marcela had been an elite volleyball player. By now, she was also an experienced orchard worker. I'd work opposite her, struggling to keep up and trying to make conversation. In Prague, she had worked as a sports journalist, interviewing Czech ice hockey heroes and other famous athletes.

Rushing to keep pace with Marcela during summer pruning, my loppers would get jammed. I'd pretend to be calm, holding in tantrums, while she patiently came back to help me with the tangle. My pruning wasn't making an impression on her and neither would my bank statement. Given her background in sports journalism I thought my sport story might make an impact. I had an excuse for being a penniless and aging student; my tertiary studies had been delayed. Three Olympic games had got in the way. Marcela eventually married me, in spite of my bank account and poor pruning skills. Luckily for me she wanted to do things, not have things.

I eventually landed a one year, fixed term teaching position but I was sentenced to Greymouth. My first year teaching full time was full on. I enjoyed the challenge and the year 7 and 8 kids loved my disciplined but fun approach. Outside of teaching I helped Marcela follow up her own Coast to Coast dream and enjoyed the fantastic mountains, tramping and kayaking, which made up for this notoriously depressing and isolated West Coast township.

Marcela had previously crewed for me in the coast to coast. The race inspired her. She was gym fit, but had never ridden a racing bike or paddled a kayak. With all the gear, the Coast to Coast doesn't come cheap, and there was now my loan to pay off. Marcela was working hard at a preschool, for peanuts. Gaining New Zealand permanent residency had also been costly and there was little to spare. We were busy now, trying to get on our feet but Marcela was efficient with her time. We spent what little we had on needs, not wants. She still made time to train, she had made a promise.

We shared the racing bike, bought a second-hand kayak and just 'bit the bullet' with the massive entry fee. We didn't need a fancy 4-wheel drive. The 20 year old Toyota and its homemade roof rack did the job. Marcela was like me, she wasn't in the sport for the fancy toys, she wanted the experience. The race was a complete success. She was worried about coming last but finished mid pack in the two day race. Her parents made a once in a lifetime visit to New Zealand at the time. We laughed, camped, waved a Czech flag all the way across Arthur's Pass National Park, and all the way to Christchurch. Marcela was a machine, everything went smoothly. I was so proud and cried when she crossed the line at Sumner Beach.

Marcela didn't go to the Olympics or break world records but the personal satisfaction for her was equally immense. Her experience was so absolutely worth the sacrifice. Satisfaction is not determined by the size of the achievement but by what must be given up to achieve it.

After my contract expired I had to settle for relief teaching. I continued to dabble in multisport without the fanatical commitment I had done as an Olympic speed skater. I had married Marcela, we had a family and a future together. But I trained when I could and in 2008 I placed 15th in the longest day event. After the Coast to Coast I was a weed. I'd get back into lifting in the winter, put on muscle and had a couple more goes at powerlifting. My diverse fitness routine was keeping me strong, keeping me fit and taking me on adventures!! I loved adventures. I became a 'jack of all trades' athlete, and the benefits of the various codes would soon prove useful assets to a bigger challenge than could possibly be imagined.

I maintained my ability on the bike with the occasional long bike ride. I once decided to up the family distance record, and rode from Greymouth to Nelson to see Chris. Showing off, with 330 km. I was NGF champion! Chris accused me having howling tailwinds. This was a lie, and I approved my record immediately.

Marcela was now being overworked and underpaid, and there were few opportunities for me to gain any full-time position. Those that did arise were given to friends of the school board. We needed a change, we dreamed of getting ahead like normal people. We desired meaningful employment, to pay off my loan, and perhaps one day get into a home of our own. Besides the fantastic surrounding nature, there was nothing for us in Greymouth.

We took 18 months to work in Britain where we both worked as relief teachers. We would never have lasted long in the grim city of Coventry but it was a chance to at least make a little money. The peace of New Zealand soon called and Marcela and I finished the trip by cycling from London to Istanbul. Marcela was amazing, averaging 150 km per day. Unbeknownst to me I was scouting ahead for a future ride I had not yet considered.

On return we tried our luck in Dunedin, it was the only place we could hope to afford a house, and luckily, we enjoyed the small South Island city. Marcela soon found employment in tourism but I continued to be shut out, occasionally being fed scraps of relief teaching.

Relief teaching was highly unrewarding. The job involves little actual teaching and lots of crowd control or behaviour management. In spite of my obvious skills, as an outsider I was kept at arm's length by the local schools. The rejection letters for full time work kept flowing.

Since my Olympic career, I had added a psychology diploma and an ESOL language teaching certificate to my teaching degree. I had also learned other languages and in recent years I had made time to enjoy and develop skills of a less physical nature. I became a competent amateur guitarist and a watercolour artist. Clearly other skills adding to my obvious value as primary school teacher.

Nonetheless I continued to be deprived of a career in favour of teachers who resembled those at University, those that fit the Kiwi mould. Was it me? Something else? It wasn't my CV, I had excellent references. I also had excellent relationships with children. Kids loved having Mr Nicholson. "I wish you could teach every day", kids would say, much to the resentment of the permanent staff.

I also sought employment outside of traditional teaching roles in community sport and exercise to no avail. My unique and unusual Olympic background didn't seem to help in the traditional New Zealand sporting culture. Potential employers saw ice skating as just a pretty novelty done by Torvill and Dean. I struggled to forgive these naive 'should have been employers' for their ignorance. I was a qualified teacher, an experienced coach, a triple Olympian; with proven performance and understanding across a diverse range of codes, from extreme strength to extreme fitness. Regardless of my qualifications and achievements, I had had a lifetime of hands on experience. My story proved without doubt that I was a driven, knowledgeable and motivated individual. It meant nothing to them. An easy out for potential employers was to label me as someone who was 'unsettled', given my unusual life story. The only reason I hadn't settled was because my country wouldn't let me settle. Catch 22. Every door was closed. I had been trying to find meaningful employment for years now. It was no surprise I was getting angry, or depressed?

Given the constant need to be in peak physical condition, I had never been a drinker, but every job rejection justified another drink. The alcohol intake was creeping up. If a clinical psychologist had assessed my situation, occasional suicidal thoughts and personality type, I would have almost certainly been diagnosed with depression. I just wanted a job! I had more than paid my dues!

"Life is like riding a bicycle. In order to keep your balance, you must keep moving"
Albert Einstein, physicist.

August 29 2014: It was a Friday afternoon and I'd been waiting for the response for a position that was made for me. Experience in PE, Music, Behaviour Management. I must have had a chance?

I'd been trying to find full time work now for six years. A meaningful profession, a chance to dig myself out of my financial mess, and settle down.

But I received a letter, not a phone call, so I knew what was coming. The letter told me that there was a high standard of applicants. Bullshit! You gave it to friend! I flew into a rage! Fuck you New Zealand! I started throwing things. I had accepted that my country would never reward or respect me for my unusual sports career. But why was I continually being deprived of the basic human right of meaningful employment. My tantrum was getting violent. I wanted to kill someone or perhaps myself, neither were good options. It wasn't fair on Marcela, I had her in tears, she felt for me but had seen this all before. This wasn't depression; this was rage! Depression usually followed a day or two later. I needed to get out. I'd escape the city for the day, take my anger out on the bike. The next morning I got up and went for a bike ride, a big one.

Chapter 5

A Big Bike Ride

In recent months, I had been too busy trying to focus on financial survival to have done any serious training. I'd jump straight into this ride. I'd leave my worries at home and complete an epic lap around central Otago. That night I prepared a full kit; warm clothes, good lights, plenty of food, and was riding by 4 am the next morning. I whipped through Dunedin, the sun still hadn't risen and the temperature was -2°C as I approached Milton. I rode through Roxburgh then over some nasty climbs, and arrived at Alexandra around midday for cakes and sausage rolls. I continued the full road loop around the outside of the rail trail and through fantastic Otago high country. After 360 km both the sun and temperature dropped as I lumbered into the town of Middlemarch. I stopped to quickly put on extra clothing and texted Chris, I was the new NGF champ. I was expecting at least a petrol station in Middlemarch and had been longing for a pie. No such luck, everything was closed and it was to be water and manky jam sandwiches over the steep hills to Mosgiel.

I wobbled into Dunedin and crawled the final 20 km, arriving at my home in Portobello around 11:30pm. 465 km! The Nicholson Grovel Ride record had been taken to a new level. I approved my application immediately. The ride had met the manliness count with plenty of hills, wind and freezing conditions. I collapsed victorious onto the bed and the ceiling became a spinning road as I fell unconscious. Marcela had to tend to my every need for the next three days.

The ride had distracted me from my unemployment situation and I was surprised how fast I'd ridden, my average riding speed was around 27 kph. I knew there was some sort of New Zealand 24 hour record out there and I did some googling. I needed a project, it would distract me from my career predicament. The ride had cheered me up. I put on the bike computer, that meant I was training. Any day when I wasn't called in to manage chaos at primary schools, I was out training, looking at the numbers. I'd break the New Zealand 24 hr record! I had new goal.

Three months after my massive grovel ride, I rode 776.1 km in one day; just under 33 kph average. Breaking the record served as a huge confidence booster. I rode 3,100 laps of the Mosgiel Velodrome.

People assumed this must have been incredibly boring but I found myself enjoying the challenge. With no distractions of traffic or hazards I was able to simply stare at the black line on the velodrome and enter a focused and smooth flow state.

Getting dizzy with 3,100 laps and 776 km in one day at the Mosgiel Velodrome

Chris came down from Nelson to support me and lent me his time trial bike for the effort. I even raised a few hundred dollars for the good people at the Otago University Cancer Research Department. Some of their researchers were active on the Otago track cycling scene. They helped organise the attempt. Riding for their cause meant more to me since I had heard that my friend Warren was dying of cancer.

I had of course also beaten the Nicholson (NGF) distance record but Chris disqualified me for a lack of manliness. The ride was done on a concrete smooth velodrome and there were no hills. The distance was impressive but it lacked any sense of adventure.

My 24 hour ride was like a win early in my skating career. I wanted more! As soon as the rush wore off I needed a bigger hit. I got out a DVD 'Bicycle Dreams', an award-winning documentary about the nonstop Race across America (RAAM). This one was for me! Tagged as the toughest race in the world, and well suited to the aged rider I was fast becoming. The financial hurdle required for RAAM, however, would be too big. Kiwi Josh Kench had recently managed the event on a shoestring budget but still spent more than $15,000 on the event. Even with a skeleton crew it still required two campervans and a minimum of five people to help crew, for up to two weeks across the USA. The financial cost would be simply too much. I could never afford to do RAAM; there just wasn't the money.

I watched 'The Man Who Cycled the World', a BBC documentary about Marc Beaumont's circumnavigation record, set in 2008. At the time, I was never considering the challenge for myself. Obviously too big, and surely out of my price range. What other epic projects could I do while waiting about? Sitting around was a death sentence and I had to keep moving or depression would catch up.

I tagged the 24hr World Championships as my next project. Unlike the Race across America, it was possibly affordable. The event is held annually in the Mojave Desert, California, and attracts a hard-core group of ultra-cyclists. A straight out 24 hour time trial, but the obscure 24 hr event would have to be self-funded and was becoming expensive. Besides, I needed something bigger and wanted to travel, not ride a few laps around a Californian desert. It might be cheaper to just ride around the world, after all? What were the rules on that circumnavigation thing again? I did some research. I already had the physical ability, the mental ability and the experience, what about the money?

I broke down the costs. Starting at the bare

minimum; needs, not wants, just like early skating trips. Firstly, I would need to get to Vancouver. An Air New Zealand special on an airfare popped up at $799. Marcela and I had enjoyed hosting a few cycle tourists and we joined an online website called Warm Showers. An online network of cycle tourists hosting other cycle tourists. With careful planning, Warm Shower hosting and camping took care of North America. I spotted an overnight special on an airfare, Boston - Lisbon $350. That was the Atlantic done. Old speed skating friends and family were also scattered evenly across my European route, and once I hit Asia, I knew from experience that I could find a bed for as little as $10 a night. Surely if I made it as far as Australia, I'd just find a way to make it? I had the body, the experience, and money wasn't going to stop me. It hadn't before. What would Marcela think? I gingerly put the question to her. She never paused. "Whatever makes you happy."

Marcela believed in me, she knew me, she felt my frustration and had faith in me. She wished me well and I booked the tickets. I'd break the world record for cycling round the planet. Game on.

"By failing to prepare, you are preparing to fail."
Benjamin Franklin

Was it possible? 125 days? I would need to

average 235 km a day, without a break and including flights. It was time to plan the detail. I started making lists and checking off steps. By financial necessity, my ride would be almost completely unsupported. I didn't bother seeking serious sponsorship, nobody would have taken me seriously, even the head of Cancer Research raised eyebrows when I suggested my plan to ride for his cause. He clearly didn't want me to become a liability. But when I outlined my plan and described my background in detail he was proud to let me ride for Cancer Research. One of his researchers, Tanis Godwin, also would serve as an essential member of what would become 'mission control', helping with online logistics. My ride would be labelled Te Aho World Ride. Te Aho Matatū, the Maori name, shows that there are entwined relationships between the CTCR, (the Centre for Translational Cancer Research) and the many communities they are working with.

I did attempt to secure bike sponsorship and was stoked when AvantiPlus Dunedin came straight to the party. Without hesitation Steve Dyet, who had followed my 24 hour ride, offered up full assistance, along with a near brand new demo bike for my ride. An Avanti Corsa DR, a semi time trial bike. It felt fantastic and Steve was happy to include my preferred choice of wheelset, Ksyrium Elite road racing wheels. Not the lightest and fastest on the road but tough and durable. They would prove to be an excellent choice. A pair of pedals from Keywin

Industries were also added. Steve also agreed to help forward chains, cassettes and tyres to designated pickup points. I was majorly appreciative, it took some of the financial strain away and gave me assurance that I was starting with top notch equipment. This would certainly limit mechanical tantrums.

Preparing the steed at Avanti Plus Dunedin, still clean and shiny

I hooked into Google Maps, Google Earth, cycle tourist blogs; and began planning my route within the Guinness rules. Route planning had to consider several factors; roads, safety, weather, visas. Africa needed to be avoided and South America would also bring numerous challenges but there was no way I could do the whole trip in 'easy countries'. I studied wind roses, probably too much. Optimal wind became an obsession, but the only predictable generalization was that traveling west to east was the best option. What about hills? Certain mountains would be unavoidable, the Rockies for example, and there was no flat way through Turkey. The Canadian Prairies were a good pick, and a flat route could be taken through most of Asia and Australia. But in remote parts of Australia I had a problem, there was nowhere to stay. A supported trip was not an option; camping was doable, and I chose to take the minimum for a night in the open, but carrying sufficient water across isolated areas of the outback would be virtually impossible. Even with minimum kit I was already looking more like a tourist than a racing cyclist. Outside my bike, my kit consisted of...

A brevet bag, a small backpack, a small inflatable sleeping mat, bivvy bag, thermal blanket, rain jacket, 2 pairs of cycling shorts, a bike jersey, a long sleeve polypropylene top, a pair of jandals, a beanie, helmet, sunglasses, first aid kit, saddle cream, spare spokes, multi tool, 2 spare tubes, repair kit, log book, GPS spot tracker, passport, phone, cash cards, lights, charger, 2 drink bottles, a light t-shirt, leg warmers, a rolled up cardboard tube containing small watercolour paintings and a cuddly toy. That's it! Speed was more important than comfort. I was trying to break a world record.

When was the best time to leave? Cycling in Canada beyond September was asking for trouble. Leaving in August would put me in Western Europe in September which was okay, and in Eastern Turkey by October. Starting to get cold, but manageable. I would then hit India just after the monsoon, and cross Australia in November to early December, hotter than ideal but also manageable. So, August was the best time to leave - but August was only three months away.

Perhaps I needed another year to seriously plan this? I considered delaying the whole project for a full year. This project was certainly a challenge better suited to an older athlete, but then, I was getting past the older athlete stage already. What if I did get a job? In another year, my passing years were likely to be a disadvantage. It was now or never. The only steady work I had was as a part-time gym instructor. I asked if my job could be put on hold. My boss was a keen ultra-runner and he immediately showed support, I would have at least something to come back to.

I sent in my proposed route to Guinness World Records as required. It was a painful wait for the result. Would it be accepted? I had an inkling that somewhere, someone else might planning an attempt? I wanted to go now!! Ultra-distance riding was becoming more popular and it would only be a matter of time before someone with a bigger budget and greater support would extend the 125 day record. Exactly two months later an email arrived from Guinness. The word 'accepted' stood out in the headline. I would make an official attempt. I paid for the air tickets.

The final training days in the Dunedin winter were repetitive but necessary. I had trained for this event my whole life without realising it, but my best chance of success was to arrive at the start line in top form. Dunedin is a great place for cycling but I had done the local rides time and time again. I wanted to travel as much as I did to break records or help a worthy cause. I specifically trained to get through long days with minimal damage. I was finishing 250 km rides and feeling fine, but whether I could do it for 125 days in a row in challenging conditions, would remain an unknown.

The adventure and travel aspect of my trip made it so much more than a normal bike race. This journey was going to be epic, and my choice to pursue it must have been in part inspired my favourite adventure story as a kid. The race to the South Pole. My dad had given me the English version, the one about the brave and patriotic Captain Robert Falcon Scott. Scott was ultimately ill-prepared, and he paid with his life. As I grew and read more about the race, I realised who the real hero of this story was. The eventual winner, and survivor, Norwegian Roald Amundsen. Captain Scott had thought he would have the race to himself but unbeknownst to him Amundsen had been secretly planning for some time. Only weeks before Scott set out he received a telegram which must have added a great deal of extra pressure:

BEG TO INFORM YOU FRAM PROCEEDING ANTARCTIC – AMUNDSEN—Telegram to Scott, ca September 9, 1910. [3]

Two weeks out from departure, I would receive a similar message. I returned from a ride to read a Facebook message from Lee Fancourt, who had kindly offered advice on this record. Another rider was also about to attempt the record. He would start just two days before me!

Peter Adam Smith from Scotland was claiming he would finish in less than 100 days. He had a professional looking website, a long list of sponsors and a huge budget. His videos and self-promotion had led to significant media attention. Apart from those directly involved, I hadn't told anyone. Before having even hit the start line, Peter had a huge online following. He also had the massive advantage of an organised crew and full support.

I knew I could get around the world quickly. I was thankful that the target average was 230 km, and not the 250 km plus that would have been required to beat Lee Fancourt and Mike Hall's unofficial records. But 100 days? This would require a daily average of 280 km! Unsupported, those distances would be surely beyond reach.

Travelling with a van and support has obvious endless benefits, the most significant being the ability to travel light. Although my set up was minimal, to say the least, it still added several kilos of unaerodynamic bulk and weight to my bike. Peter wouldn't even have to carry a water bottle.

About the only thing Peter would have to do, other than pedal, was poop. My ride still went largely by the wild man category. Having support would also eradicate many of the logistical challenges. Finding and preparing food, navigation and bike maintenance are simply left to the crew. Luxuries such as massage and emotional support were also available to Peter. This all amounts to a massive daily bonus. As far as budgets go, this was a David versus Goliath battle. It wasn't fair, but then, it had never been fair.

Controlling the controllable; I tried to avoid any deep analysis of Peter's attempt and I had certainly had come too far to consider withdrawing, yet I couldn't help looking a little deeper into his background. Despite the confidence he showed in his video presentations, I couldn't find any real evidence of Peter's success as a cyclist. Being well funded and supported was an essential piece of the puzzle, but even with support, you needed to be a good cyclist to pull off the required daily distance. Perhaps this was the essential piece missing in Peter's arsenal? Potential cracks in his physical ability also showed up in that he had already cancelled a recent attempt after only two weeks. His restart would begin on August 10, just two days before my departure.

My official start was organised for 12th August, 6 pm, outside Auckland International Airport. I now had a race to deal with as well as a record. The ride had become a 29,000 km pursuit, with riders starting on opposite sides of the planet. Both Peter and I would use the most excellent software provided by Tedde de Boer's 'followmychallenge' website. The software not only provided live tracking for both riders from our spot trackers, but also daily average, weather conditions, average speed and even street view. For online spectators, this was going to be a great online spectacle. Who would win? and would either rider break Alan Bate's record?

I boarded the flight from Dunedin to Auckland on the morning of my official start. Marcela dropped me off without fuss but I had tears in my eyes as we said goodbye. We discussed the possibility of meeting in Perth. If money could be found, perhaps she could support me across part of Australia. My last words were "thanks for letting me chase this, Baby, I need to go". She kissed me with no signs of doubt or fear in her eyes and said goodbye. Marcela had more belief in me than I did in myself.

I was collected at Auckland airport a few hours before my official start, by Jennie Clague, a friend who held the Hauraki Ice Racing Club together. Jennie had shown to be really organised and proactive with keeping the speed skating club together. She was the type to get things done quickly, was computer savvy and had time on her hands. A couple of weeks earlier I had asked her if she could perhaps help me online, with logistics, while I was peddling. Coordinate the Warm Showers hosts, booking air tickets, "it wouldn't be much", I had said. She hesitated a little before agreeing, perhaps realising correctly that this task would involve a great deal more than I was anticipating. She probably also worried about making errors and feeling responsible for my safety, which was never the case. Only I would be responsible for the success of this challenge, it was my choice.

Jennie organised the official start as per Guinness rules. Timekeepers and two solicitors were needed to act as official witnesses for my start. We set up an official start, 100 metres from the entrance to the international departure check in area. My friend Igor was there with his family, plus Jennie, her husband Philip and four officials (including Matthew Biggs, who acted as a timekeeper). Rounding out the group was a rep. from Avanti, who set up a start banner. This small group made up my send-off party.

I thought back to the clip I'd seen of Peter Adam Smith setting off down a starting ramp in front of large crowd of sponsors, onlookers and cameras. An announcer on a loudspeaker set him on his way, with well-wishers enthusiastically waving British flags. What a contrast! Philip filmed the start on an iPad, gave me a countdown, and followed me the 100m to the entrance at the departure check in. The clock on the departures board read: 6:12pm, August 12, 2015. The race was underway! I boxed up my bike, waved goodbye to the small group and boarded the flight to Vancouver.

Chapter 6

The Rockies

"It is the unknown around the corner that turns my wheels."
Heinz Stucke, long-distance touring cyclist.

I would spend the first 13 hours of my race losing time by sitting on a plane. I watched a movie 'Wild' starring Reese Witherspoon. A true story about a young, ill-prepared woman who 'finds herself' as she hikes alone on the Pacific Crest Trail in Western USA. I thought it ironic that I was undertaking a far more impressive and 'wild' journey, knowing it would likely never be made into an award-winning movie.

DAY 1. After exiting customs, at around 3 pm local time, I excitedly assembled my bike outside Vancouver Airport. The clock was ticking! The last few training rides I did in Dunedin, I wore full winter kit and there had been snow on the hills. The afternoon warmth felt fantastic. I assembled my bike outside Terminal 2 in a balmy 25°C.

By 4pm I was riding! One kilometre down and 28,999 to go. The traffic lights and industrial areas of Vancouver were an eyesore but I couldn't believe I had actually started. I made my way over the Alex Fraser bridge through thick rush hour traffic.

Cruising at speed during a brief suburban downhill section, I made a sweeping left turn... checking right. A car screeched to a halt missing me by inches. I couldn't believe what I had just done! I had looked the wrong way and got away with it. This idiotic mistake was so close to being an embarrassing 20 km trip ending in Vancouver Hospital. What a moron!...note to self, Canada drives on the right.

After 81 km of working my way through the outer Vancouver suburbs I approached the town of Abbotsford, close to the Fraser river. I had been here before, 25 years earlier I had spent time with kind hosts while I skated with local clubs.

My first Warm Showers hosts for the night were Brian and Taraleigh. They typified the fantastic people I would meet through the Warm Showers site. Brian fed me burritos then led me to a comfortable basement suite complete with a warm shower. Brian could see my enthusiasm for what lay ahead and questioned me as to whether I thought the same energy would be present in one, two or even three months' time. I wondered the same thing.

Getting immediately into the important habit of an early start, I was ready with my bike by 5:15am for my first full day. Brian was also on the way out to his early shift at the prison where he worked as a guard. He shook my hand and wished me well. The sun was rising and I was massively excited. The race had finally begun in earnest, I'd slept well and my first full day lay ahead.

The Trans-Canadian Highway approaching the Rockies had a smooth riding surface and ample shoulder, but the large amount of metal debris scattered in the shoulder required focus. Various bolts, pieces of chain and shredded chunks of tyre required constant attention. It was inevitable, given the large amount of trucking transport that crosses this massive continent.

The mountains grew closer as I made my way through the green Fraser Valley toward the town of Hope, which lay at the bottom of the first serious climb. *'This.sss. sss.ss....'* clipping an unidentifiable piece of steel, I had received puncture number one. I swore and called the puncture gods some rude names. I wanted to get moving! I considered hurling my bike into a bush as well, but it was way too early for a full-scale tantrum. Knowing that punctures would be an inevitable part of the journey, I took a deep breath and then calmly changed my first tube, forgiving the puncture gods and apologising for my obscenities.

I soon realised I had made a mistake in choosing a vital piece of equipment. It took a huge effort to get any reasonable amount of pressure into my tyre with my tiny emergency pump. I hadn't properly tested this pump. Saving weight and space was essential in covering such massive distances so I had opted for a discreet and small hand pump. What I really needed was a good old fashioned lengthy thruster. The old school type that easily snaps under the top tube. I hunched over my bike and began pumping vigorously. Bent over the wheel, to the passing truckers I must have looked like I was frantically masturbating. Even after several minutes and 500 thrusts later I still had barely 80 pounds pressure, in a tyre designed for 120. Finally I continued beyond Hope, on what appeared to be the main Highway, where the flat riding of the Fraser Valley was about to come to an end.

The first major climbs of the Rocky Mountains lay immediately ahead. Kamloops was North and my planned host for the night was expecting me. 200 km straight up the main highway, easy. I hadn't felt the need to pay too much attention to my navigation at this stage. I assumed I would just head north up the mountain on the most obvious double divided highway. I climbed for over an hour in brutal heat, surprised by the thinning of traffic. The road was still big by New Zealand standards but soon narrowed to a single lane in each direction. There were few signs. Finally I noticed a road sign, and it said...Highway 3.

To my horror, I realised I'd been going the wrong way! 40 km the wrong way, up a mountain. I considered backtracking, but the Guinness people would subtract the kilometres and then I'd still have 200 km to get to Kamloops. I chose to ride on. After only one day I had screwed up my whole schedule. The route had changed, I would now head east via the Princeton Highway. Destination: Princeton.

I managed to get a text out to cancel my host and kept climbing and descending through the stunning alpine wilderness of the more remote Highway 3. The temperature kept rising, sapping my strength. Sure, it was summer, but this was Canada? The Canada I'd known was one of snow, ice and cold. It hit 37°C and the brutal climbs kept coming, some nearly 2000m. My body was used to the Dunedin winter and I wasn't coping with the heat. In spite of pumping in fluid I was badly cramping. I eventually rode my required 232 km and rolled into the scenic mountain town of Princeton. I picked up some surprisingly expensive groceries and camped beside a gorgeous mountain river.

I hadn't expected to use my emergency 'night out' gear this early in the trip, but due to the massive navigational cock up, I would have to camp. Affordable accommodation was not an option. Camping? That would have implied putting up a tent. I slipped into what was marketed as a Bivvy Bag, but what in reality was a canvas sheet. I shuffled down to try and sleep. Although I was on the outskirts of town, I had seen bear warning signs, and every bump in the night had to be a bear.

I'd nearly gotten squashed in Vancouver, chosen the wrong pump and certainly the wrong bivvy bag. I'd taken the wrong road and was already trashed. Over the coming months I would need to navigate through some of the world's largest and most confusing cities. But only on Day 2, differentiating between State Highway 1 and 3 had proved too difficult. I felt like a complete nong! It had not been a great first full day. What was I doing? Doubt set in and I fought to beat it back. Had I bitten off more than I could chew? Was I ill-prepared? Or had I just had a sequence of misfortunate events?

I spent a few hours between shivering and overheating, all the while jumping at bear noises. After about two hours of unsettled sleep it was time to ride. On top of the disastrous second day, I was still recovering from a man flu I'd picked up before departure. I set off, already feeling trashed on the now altered plan. The less direct Highway 3 would put my schedule out, but I managed to get hold of Jennie with the instruction to re-organise all the pre-booked hosts. This wouldn't be the first job that Jennie would be flooded with.

I had underestimated the traffic and population of inland British Columbia. On Day 3 I hit the height of the US and Canadian holiday traffic, heading home in both directions for the start of another school year. I hadn't been in Canada for years and everything seemed big; roads, people, and particularly, vehicles and RVs. Some of these holiday trailers carried a whole house. They had equally massive names like 'Prowler' and 'Bounty Hunter', all being towed by massive 4x4s called 'The Beast' or 'The Avenger'! Many of them were loaded with jet skis, quad bikes and other noise polluting toys. I found this all kind of ironic, considering my idea of the outdoors is peace and quiet?

I found a tourist information centre in Penticton who booked me into the only affordable accommodation, down the road in Kelowna. I needed a bed after the night of bear terror.

I stayed in the Kelowna Youth Hostel. The scene had changed since a generation ago when I stayed in hostels on skating trips. The common room was no longer a place of international exchanges using actual words. Young people from all over the world lounged lazily on couches, staring into smartphones and oblivious to the real people beside them. I was probably the oldest one there, but certainly the fittest. I stuffed my face with noodles, put in the ear plugs, and popped a pill. Three days down, well over a hundred to go... I quickly reframed the thought. I had already done three days! A motivating trick I had learned was to recognise what you had already done, rather than what lay ahead. I was asleep within seconds.

I crept out the door in the darkness, passing an international snoring contest, and later that morning re-joined the Trans-Canada Highway. I was headed for the mountain town of Revelstoke, in the heart of the Rockies. At this stage of the trip I was still managing time for a strict 30 minute stretch in the afternoon. I stopped at The Last Spike, the historical point at which the Trans Canada Railways East and West workers hammered in the last spike, making the movement of goods and people possible across this massive continent. Not unlike New Zealand, this railway not only boosted development, it also left both countries with a fantastic Alpine Tourist attraction.

I had arranged to stay with a Warm Showers host named Maurice, a depressing and balding French Canadian living out West. I appreciated the room and mattress, but Maurice was somewhat negative toward my challenge. "Why are youz trying to do it in five min? You won't zee anything. You will never make it to Canmore tomorrow".

My body had recovered and settled somewhat, after the torturous Day 2 on the Princeton Highway. It was time to get chasing that record. I excused myself from Maurice's lectures and prepared for a massive 330 km day to Canmore. I used his negativity as motivation, I needed to start picking up my average. I hadn't put too much thought into the record at this stage.

I was riding by 5am and climbed for couple of hours out of Revelstoke. This pristine environment of the Canadian Rockies is like an adult version of Arthur's Pass, the scenery was like New Zealand's Southern alps, upsized. Mountain peaks, glaciers, lakes, waterfalls, and canyons, all forming a striking mountain landscape that would be an impossible act to follow.

Racing the Rockies, artist's impression.
By Andrew Nicholson

I rode on some impressive feats of road engineering, bigger versions of the Otira Viaduct and avalanche tunnels that carved their way through mountain passes. Even the local history mirrors that of New Zealand's West Coast Gold Rush. A mad dash to get overland through to the west; to where prosperity apparently awaited. It would be some time before I would see water this clear again. The pristine environment of Western Canada certainly equals New Zealand. I crossed the turquoise waters of Canadian's Columbia River.

As I headed towards Canmore, the traffic increased. A horn blasted from the opposite direction. I instantly recognised my old friend Mike Bentley, who still sported a white beard that would impress Santa. Mike and his wife Laura and their now adult son Chris had been tracking me. They had hosted me on skating trips 15 years earlier, helping make my long track dream a reality. They swung about to begin helping me on another project. After a brief catch up, Mike took my bags and I continued riding. My bike felt super light, I had a tailwind and I relaxed knowing Mike would track me safely to Canmore. I was loving the journey and pounded up what was the highest point of the trip. I was already over the continental divide and heading downhill to Boston.

After a feast at a fast food joint with the Bentleys, I popped around the corner to my Warm Showers host. Sheila was a bubbly cycling enthusiast and I wasn't her only guest for the night. Andrew and Amanda were a Canadian couple, also on one hell of an epic cycle tour, traveling the full length of the Americas and taking as long as they liked. What a memorable day. I'd ridden a massive 330 km over a couple of massive mountain passes, met old friends and made new ones. I remembered every moment. A fantastic day. I thought about Warren.

The next day I exited the Rockies and headed for Calgary where I had plenty of old contacts. I had lived in Calgary on and off between 1994 and 2000. The distance lost in the short 120 km day would have to be made up for elsewhere. I couldn't miss the nostalgia of revisiting the place where I had realised the final chapter of my childhood skating dream.

Chapter 7

Underdog

"The fact of being an underdog changes people in ways that we often fail to appreciate. It opens doors and creates opportunities and enlightens and permits things that might otherwise have seemed unthinkable."
Malcolm Gladwell

It was obvious that the relay team would disband after our sad demise at the 1994 Lillehammer Olympics. Our achievements in the early 1990s would become lost to history. The days of New Zealand having a world class team were over before anyone in New Zealand ever had noticed. I would be left to compete as an individual skater. It would be back to the lonely road of training alone for individual results. I also could have retired, my 1983 vision had *sort of* come true... I'd twice made it to the Olympics, *and* been on the Weet-Bix box. But I was way too young to submit to drudgery. Besides, I wanted more travel. I considered adapting to another sport, cycling perhaps, like Chris?

But my dream as a 12 year old was quite clear. I was competing in *long* track speed skating; like in the videos we'd been watching on my first skating trip. My name was on the results board in a big outdoor, alpine stadium, it was snowing. The board said NICHOLSON NZL. I can't remember the ranking or the time. Chris had woken me up late for school.

Long Track (400m track) is the original version of speed skating. There are no tracks in New Zealand. With deep traditions, it was included in the very first Winter Olympics of 1924. The first World Championships were held way back in 1889. Popular in many Northern European countries and parts of Asia, by 1994 professionalism was already established at the top end. In Holland, the sports elite carried rock star status and like most of the world's best in long track, they were full time athletes.

Short track had been included for the first time in the 1992 Olympics. Compared to long track, it was still in its infancy. Making the change would be the equivalent of changing from sevens rugby to super rugby. Long track had numbers, particularly in Holland where traditionalists scoffed at short track, viewing it in much the same way as my grandfather viewed one-day cricket. Short track was a tough sport but long track was going to be a step up.

I was up for the challenge. I'd make the switch.

I would attempt to qualify for the 1998 Nagano Olympics. If successful, I would become the first Kiwi Long Track Olympian.

Making it backpacker style would be a challenge. Unfazed, I immediately set about getting access to a facility. The closest thing New Zealand had to offer was natural ice at Lake Ida in Central Canterbury. From the 1960s to the mid '80s long track races had been held on this lake, which for a few weeks in winter would freeze, occasionally. On mid-winter weekends dozens of cars would make a chilly two hour journey over gravel roads from Christchurch. Organised races were held annually, but by the 1990s, after series of poor winters, the federation gave up hosting outdoor or 'long track' events. The lake eventually became off limits to the public.

Training at lake Ida was difficult. Firstly, my unwarranted Datsun 180b wouldn't make the drive. A couple of times I'd been able to borrow a car, climb a fence then hike to the dangerously thin patches of ice that hadn't been covered in snow. Given that I was hoping to be the first New Zealander to qualify for the Olympics, I needed a better facility.

In August 1994, I quit my job at a bike shop and left New Zealand indefinitely. The start was going to be made on the cheap. By putting all my eggs in one basket I could maybe afford to do one season. The then Sports Foundation hadn't completely given up on me after Lillehammer. A few thousand dollars had been allocated based on my short track results. I headed for Calgary. I didn't tell the sports foundation that I was going to try long track, they wouldn't have known the difference.

Calgary was the host city of the 1988 Winter Olympics and is home to the University of Calgary Olympic Oval. This fantastic facility was the world's fastest speed skating track. A modern, multipurpose, state of the art indoor facility. A perfectly maintained 400m track surrounded the two full sized hockey rinks in the centre. Athletics track, pool and weights room are attached, along with other facilities designed for producing Canada's best athletes. The Oval, as it was known, was used as a training base for numerous Canadian and international athletes. It was without doubt the best place for me to begin my long track campaign. It was a big step up from the Paradice Ice Rink in Auckland and somewhat more dependable than Lake Ida.

I rented a tiny basement suite near the track and continued to live by the 'needs not wants' style, and set about learning to skate in a whole new way. I made some great friends with many local and international skaters who had also made Calgary home, in search of glory or for the love of the sport.

Besides the far larger track, long track races are run in a completely different format. The races are run in pairs and all races are straight out time trials. Skaters are in separate lanes and change each lap from the inner to the outer lane to balance the distance. The straights are long; the lanes are wide. There is room to simply skate unimpeded. All that matters is time. World class long track skaters gracefully lope down long straights in a picture of efficiency. Their style seems effortless and relaxed. I had developed the necessary physical conditioning but you need to be technically smooth in long track skating, I most certainly was not.

I had been racing short track, which was about never ending corners. On the edge stuff, first across the line. Buzzing around a tiny 111 metre track, skaters jockey closely for position for the first few laps. As the pace increase skaters hang on extreme angles, tussling elbow to elbow in a dash to get the foot over the line. I was a scrappy skater and even in short track I compensated with strength and fitness.

While I watched world class long track skaters floating along I was hacking and thrashing my way down the long straights. I bounced up and down like a yo yo with my blades noisily tearing large chunks out of the ice behind me. My faults were obvious; I paid an American coach what I could afford for some technical coaching. We worked hard to improve my technique but my old short track habits were hard to break.

Nonetheless, my short track background and cycling fitness was proving to be a most definite asset. Despite the hacking I made a positive start in the mid to long distance races of 1500 and 5000 metres. I was soon producing surprisingly good times in weekly training races. What I lacked in finesse I compensated for with powerful lungs and legs. I was well trained from short track. I continued to train hard. Both on and off the ice I undertook punishing sessions daily, as was required.

I took the risk of spending what little money I had on being a full-time skater. This meant the usual sacrifices. No frills, I had enough to pay the rent, live cheaply. Naturally I rode my bike everywhere, increasingly risky as the snow began to settle in the long Canadian winter. For the moment, I needed to get through the first season with at least some results, and possibly some funding might continue. Just like in short track I was being the best I could be with the resources available. I was giving it my best shot, period. Giving it my best meant way beyond simply training hard. I would eat as best as was possible, stretch, visualise. I would leave no stone unturned. If you give it your best, there is no failure.

I had a long way to go before Nagano. But if the clock told me I was progressing; I was on track. Despite my sloppy technique I was soon achieving the World Cup qualifying times and within a few months I headed off to Europe for the first round of

World Cup events. New Zealand would have its first genuine competitor in long track speed skating.

The first World Cup was held in Berlin, specifically former East Berlin, at the Sports Hallen Training Complex. The numerous facilities and sports stadiums took up a large area in this depressing part of the city. The wall may have been down for five years but change had been slow to arrive, concrete and drab was still popular. After Calgary everything seemed grotty, the maintenance man had clearly been fired the day the wall came down.

The Sports Hallen Complex was home to the dubious system for former East German athletic development. It was here behind the wall that athletes were forced onto government sponsored drug programs. Speed skaters were included in the drive to display the superiority of Soviet Bloc athletes. On this very spot gallons of steroids had been injected into many of the former East German skaters, who were still competing. They still carried manly physiques, scars from acne explosions and spoke with deep scary voices. The German women in particular favoured muscle over technique.

Jetlagged and weary from my flight from Canada I entered the dimly lit 'athlete's hotel'. The lobby and reception had an ugly 1960s décor, most things were broken, it was a dump. Other skaters in international tracksuits and team wear were milling around the lobby of gloom. My jacket said New

Zealand Short Track. It was the one item from the Lillehammer Olympics that I hadn't sold for funding. I drew some stares. Long track skaters didn't follow short track. It was beneath them; they hadn't heard of me.

The hotel stank! It was an athlete's hotel, but smoking was permitted in the lobby. The numerous East European officials hanging around on free trips showed little concern for the lungs of their athletes, puffing away furiously on cigars. The skating track was indoors but was basic compared to Calgary. Known as 'The Factory', things were made to be practical for the athletes, not enjoyable.

It took some time to convince the miserable looking receptionist that I was the New Zealand Speed Skating Team. After demanding payment, eventually she slapped a key on the desk and shooed me off to the 4th floor. Rooms resembled prison cells. By taking away comforts, perhaps it was thought the athletes would find training more enjoyable. The Dutch and other well-funded nations didn't stay here. They could afford more comfortable accommodation.

The lift creaked and groaned and I questioned its maintenance record. The doors eventually opened and who should appear but none other than Kiwi Olympic swimming champion Danyon Loader! Danyon was in Berlin for a swimming meet. We briefly chatted, but he was in as much of a hurry to get out of Berlin as I was to get some much-needed sleep. Two Kiwi Olympians on similar missions whose paths crossed briefly, a long way from the contrasting paradise of our home.

For the following three weekends, I would compete in my first Long Track World Cups. Like most Winter Olympic sports, a series was held over the season. I skated well in Berlin, placing 29th in a large field of the world's best. Immediately after the event the teams from other nations took the short flight to Holland. By mid-Monday they were cosied up in their 4-star hotel for the next week of preparation. I was still hanging around Berlin waiting to a hitch a lift across Germany with a kind Dutch official. A flight wasn't in the budget. I spent the week staying with skating fans I met in Berlin. The official hotel was only paid for during the three nights of competition.

Again, I skated well in Heerenveen where I experienced the party atmosphere of the packed Dutch skating halls for the first time. The following weekend a 3rd World Cup was scheduled for Bergan in the fjords of Norway, but I wouldn't be going. I didn't have the funds. I was on a high from my first major event, yet at the same time, sad to be missing Bergen. But as I was packing my bags to return to Calgary, the hotel phone rang. The receptionist had a call for me from Norway.

The Norwegian Organising Committee enquired as to why I wouldn't be attending this event. I explained that the cost of an extra flight to

Norway was simply out of the question. The New Zealand Ice Racing Federation didn't have the money and I was only just surviving on a small and rapidly diminishing Sports Foundation grant.

Recognising me as a potential draw card, 'The exotic skating creature from down under', the committee used their own funding to get me to the event. Eight months earlier, Norwegian Johann Olav Koss had won three Olympic golds for Norway, but in the Berlin and Heerenveen world cups the Norwegians had underperformed. There had been a scathing article in the Norwegian press. Members of their team had been beaten by a short tracker from down under. Had I been beating Norwegians already? The committee flew me to Bergen where I was put in a 4-star hotel for the week before the event. Again, I skated well and turned some heads, placing 19th in the 5000m. My race was shown live on Eurosport where the commentators had to fill in seven minutes about a skater from New Zealand that they had never heard of. I was treated like royalty. The organising committee even bought me a new ticket to fly me back to Calgary as the original couldn't be changed. I was having a blast!

I returned to Calgary for a further six weeks training before the next goal. Outside it was getting brutally cold, but on the indoor Olympic track I continued to train hard. The world championships were soon to be held in the Italian Alps, on an outdoor track in the winter sports town of Baselga Di Pinè; 'Baselga'.

To get to Baselga I began by catching the sky train to Calgary Airport. The Canadian team turned up for a different flight just as I was boarding. I took the cheapest overnight flight I could find, complete with a screaming child, to London. After a two hour transfer I boarded for Frankfurt. It was the closest city I could afford near Baselga. About 1,200 km. Clearing customs, I found a train heading south to the Italian city of Trento. With a couple of train changes, it took a full day to get to Trento. The journey took me through some stunning areas of the Alps, through the Brenner pass and past the sharp peaks of the Dolomites. I was excited about this event. The world all round champs were the pinnacle of speed skating. This was the biggest event on the international calendar. I was confident, skating well, and after two days of planes, trains and automobile, I was nearly there!

The organising committee had forgotten to pick me up. I bumped into an American tourist and we agreed to split the cost of cheap hotel room. I was trashed, I'd do the final 3O km tomorrow. I was asleep the moment my head hit the pillow.

The next day I was picked up and driven up a series of alpine switchbacks to the official hotel opposite the track. I had made it! Later that day I attended my first training session just as the Canadian team were finishing their second. Their association had flown them directly to Milan where they were whipped straight to the official hotel. They had beaten me by a day! The preparation for the biggest event of the year was less than ideal, but I had got there!

While I lumbered around the track jetlagged, ground staff and volunteers were busy erecting the extra stands required to cater for the thousands of mostly Dutch fans whose arrival in town was imminent. Mobs of singing orange clad supporters had already arrived; a real festival atmosphere was well underway. The Dutch were the best at this sport, they could be as loud as they liked.

While I trained, large flags of the competing nations were being hung above the extra seating that was hastily being erected. That the New Zealand flag was absent was of no surprise but hanging between the skating super powers of the Netherlands and Norway was the familiar flag of Australia. I knew my alphabet, and I also knew there were no Australians at this event. The Italian organising committee hadn't got around to updating their flag collection. Australia would have to do.

The following day I noticed an attempt had been made to solve the flag issue. Some nearly matching blue paint had been splashed over the extra stars on the Australian flag. Nobody would notice, and apart from me nobody did notice. The flag alteration might offend a few Kiwis but I just thought it was funny. For me it highlighted the fact that I had made it in a sport where no Kiwi should ever have made it.

Like the World Cups and like the early short track days, I would attend coach-less. Having no coach was absurd in the short track world, but in long track the idea was unheard of. This was a World Championship, but there was no funding in the budget for a New Zealand Coach. There wasn't even enough for me. The long track scene meant living outside New Zealand, numerous trips for World Cups, lots of flight tickets. I would have to survive alone, but then, I was used to coaching myself.

By now I had become friends with some of the Canadian team who also trained in Calgary. Their team coach kindly passed on anything relevant from the official's team meetings; training times, race draw etc. I got the information I needed, but I was given the impression by the more pompous officials that my perceived amateurism made the sport look bad.

Although I could certainly have benefited from some professional support, I took pride in having made it alone. The ISU officials may not have approved of my solo, budget style appearance, but the Dutch media thought my story was cool. Intrigued by the sudden appearance of a competitive skater from down under, I gave several interviews explaining my background in Short Track. The sport of long track attracts statistics nuts. People were often asking my personal bests, about New Zealand, Lake Ida, records etc.

An hour or so before the start of the first race the stadium was already in party mode. A large Oompah band kept spectators warm with singing and dancing. Many of the Dutch had hit their hip flasks and Heineken early. With the media attention, it seemed I'd even attracted a few fans, banners wishing me well were waved from fans I'd never met.

It was fantastic to know that I had already made an impression. Back home it was cricket season but other than my old team mates, nobody in New Zealand had a clue what I was up to. I was competing on the biggest stage in the sport of speed skating. The modified Australian flag made me proud. The videos I watched in 1983 had sparked a dream that had led to the sacrifices necessary to make it happen. It even looked like it was going to snow.

The All-round World Championships are raced over four distances: 500m, 1500m, 5000m and 10000m; each counting equally towards the total. The event begins with the 500 metres, an all-out sprint. The early pairs were setting fast times and I was paired with Polish skater Jaromir Radke, who had placed 5th in the previous Olympics in the

5000m. Radke wasn't a serious contender overall however, famous for his complete absence of fast twitch fibres. The starter called to us to the line, "Go to the start". I may have been new to long track but through Craig Lewis and years of short track I could handle the pressure. I was fully focused. Compared to the close quarter danger of short track racing, long track was mentally easy. Just you, your lane and a race against the clock.

The starter's gun cracked and the intense roar of the crowd followed me down the starting straight. Radke accelerated like my old Datsun wouldn't and disappeared, he was making me look good. I was skating well, in the zone and only momentarily distracted from a minor stumble a few steps into the race. With adrenaline pumping and in the zone, I crossed the line in a respectable 27th place. I suddenly became aware of pain in my right ankle. The stumble may have cost me little time but had caused serious damage. My blade had neatly sliced my ankle.

Just above the boot line, blood was dripping steadily behind me, forming a puddle on the ice as I glided to a stop. My first Long Track World Championships looked over, only moments after it had begun. I needed a doctor but my New Zealand team didn't even have a coach. The Canadian Doctor Ingrid looked, and her face confirmed my suspicions. The ankle needed stitching. Committed to her own skaters, the best she could do was point me to the Italian Red Cross.

The Red Cross Team were busy in the stands dealing with a head injury from a Dutch spectator named Henk. Henk had started drinking early that morning and missed most of the 500m, he had fallen on the icy stands trying to find his way back to his seat.

Medics lead us to a Fiat Ambulance which whipped us down the mountainside to a local First Aid Centre, Henk slurring a patriotic Dutch song along the way. An attractive Italian first aider named Maria attended to my bleeding. The 5000m event was about two hours away and if I didn't race I would be disqualified. I had just sliced my ankle open with a speed skating blade. Continuing the event seemed unlikely.

Communication with the first aiders was difficult. The gorgeous Maria, like the rest of the team, spoke no English. After a brief examination, a seemingly busy doctor began preparing a cord to begin work on my ankle. I mimed a request for some form of local aesthetic but the good doctor deemed it unnecessary. He set to work, waving me away as a wuss? I anticipated pain! Maria also seemed surprised at the doctor's call and grimaced, clutching me to her ample bosom for comfort. Henk vomited.

The doctor hooked into my ankle as if he were darning an old pair of socks. It hurt but Maria's bosom got me through the worst of the pain. Four stitches later Maria was left to wipe up both my blood and Henk's vomit.

My biggest concern was getting back to the track in time to race the 5000m. I mimed a question to the doctor, my ankle hurt but could I skate on it? The doctor sternly shook his head. My heart sank, my first world champs looked over after only one event. I was taken back to the stadium, back to where the first pairings of the 5000 metres had already begun. It had started to snow. My dream from 1983 was playing out. My name was on the scoreboard. I was due on in about 30 min but had resigned to withdrawing. I showed the doctor's handy work to Ingrid, seeking a more positive professional opinion. She knew what I had sacrificed to get here, and said, "The worst that can happen is needing to go back for further stitching." That was all I needed to hear. I warmed up, focused, stepped out; and demolished my Korean pairing, placing 21st. Some of the superstar Dutch and Norwegians had respect, they had heard my story and seen me bleeding earlier. They high-fived me as I exited the ice; I was immensely proud.

I continued to improve for the remainder of the 94-95 season, even producing the ninth fastest time in the world over the season in the 3000 metres. I had met the high expectations I had set for myself and made an excellent start to the long track code. I had good reason to be confident that I would more than qualify for the 1998 Olympics but had no idea of the struggles I would face before Nagano.

Chapter 8

Into The Great Wide Open

On August 22 2015 I was met outside the Olympic Oval by my old friend Arno, a professional skating coach. Arno had attended three Olympics as a coach. He was fantastic crew and gave me a tour of changes to the Oval. The environment was much the same. The echo of international language from coaches rang around the stadium. International short track and long track squads of skaters were being put through structured routines, both on and off the ice. Korean athletes were still being barked at and threatened with beatings. New testing machines and modern training tools had been added. Especially cameras, used by staff to assess the skater's form, from every possible angle. The athletes were no longer people, they were products of a system. The sport had evolved a further notch as reflected in recent world records. Arno led me back to his place for a huge feed and much needed sleep.

At sunrise I passed the hospital where 22 years earlier my ankle had had to be re-stitched, a few weeks after the Italian incident. I left Calgary and the mountains behind, entering the Canadian Prairies.

The Canadian Prairies extend for around 3,000 km, not entirely flat, but they are vast!! Rolling hills of wheat field and nothing fields disappear into the distant horizon. The Canadian Prairies bring a sense of scale that can't be felt back home. In New Zealand it's never long before the scenery changes. We also have plains and tons of open space, but there's always something on the horizon in New Zealand; a mountain, a farmhouse, lake or a coastline. Even Central Otago seemed tiny compared to the eerie emptiness of the world's second biggest country. Apart from the corridor of the wide Trans-Canada Highway, there was nothing in any direction. Looking north, I realised that the landscape continued uninterrupted for thousands of kilometres, with virtually no habitation. I couldn't help thinking about the early wagon trains, moving west into this emptiness, the journey must have seemed endless.

At 3 o'clock I saw a tree and had a party. The landscape is not beautiful in the traditional sense, but with little change on the horizon I would tend to look upwards and notice the stunning cloud formations, the vastness and changing light displaying its own type natural beauty. You just have to look for it. Mike Bentley had put me on to some friends of his in Medicine Hat. They treated me like a king.

The scenery over the next few days continued to look like the background in a Flintstones cartoon. Entering Saskatchewan I had still yet to meet a cycle tourist, until I came across a Frenchman (who was actually named Pierre). He had stopped and tucked himself behind a wheat belt for protection against the wind. Pierre was trying to start a wood fire without wood, and looked like he'd been having an Andrew tantrum. I swung about to say hi. He was friendly enough and I asked about his trip. Pierre had had a tough time, fighting the headwind that had beaten him for 2 months. I quietly hoped it would last for a little longer, I was enjoying the tailwind. Predominant westerlies for the moment.

"I sink Canada iza very boring" he said. "Two months I have been fighting thez shet!" Pierre would soon change his mind, within a few days he would be in the paradise of the Rocky Mountains and I hoped his headwind slog across the plains would have been worth it.

Approaching Moose Jaw a car slowed beside me, the passenger an older lady with a friendly smile who held a sign, 'Hi Andrew, friend of James McKellar, coffee?' James was a friend I knew through cycling in Dunedin, he had been a major helper and organiser of my 24 hour record. James had been following me online and sent out support; Roy and Marie had been tracking me. They kindly took me in for a shower and food before I found my way to my pre-arranged host for the night.

A warm showers host named Keri gave me a bed that night. Keri had started an awesome venture. She would tend the gardens of locals using organic methods. I employed my primary school skills and enjoyed reading her son a book while she pottered around with vegetables and potted plants. Another kind stranger.

A super early 4am start was needed for Day 9. It was to be a whopper. I was peddling, still half asleep, when not long after leaving Moose Jaw I was jolted into a sprint. A wild coyote had started pacing alongside me in the darkness. I 'beep beeped' as best I could and it took me some time at 45kph to lose the beast. I found myself suddenly awake and alert. As I slowed down I started to wonder if the coyote was on the internet now, ordering some kind of ACME rocket booster?

Other than a brief fast food and Supermarket shop at Regina I would be on the bike for nearly 16 hours on day 9. At this stage, other than a constantly aching neck, my body was holding up. Given the flat terrain, I was spending nearly all the time on the aerobars. It is in this position that my neck would ache most.

Following the Race across America I'd read about the numerous cases of 'Shermer's neck', a condition common in the nonstop race where nerves and muscles argue. Once the condition begins you are stuck with it, and the rider eventually becomes unable to support his own head. Riders in RAAM often either end up retiring, or getting their heads braced or taped into position, to stay in the race.

I set to MacGyvering, mangling a drink bottle and duct taping it in an upright position from the handle bars stem, using it as a support. A discarded polystyrene Chinese takeaway box served as padding, and voila! A neck rest. It worked well. The ache in the neck subsided but it was an epic day. The wind had turned to the side and progress was slow. The speedometre was reading in the low twenties, it was going to be a long, long day.

Many people complain about riding on the aero bars. Perhaps it is the bike set up, a weak back or poor posture, but I am at home and most comfortable in this position. It is faster and more comfortable. Apart from serious climbs and hopping about in cities I would spend 70% of my day in this position. The strength, good posture and flexibility I had developed over the years enabled me to ride in a comfortable and aero position all day.

In Saskatchewan I passed a nothing town called Whitewood, Population 209. I began to wonder what the hell keeps people going out here in the long cold winter months. Snow covers the ground from as early as October and can stick around right through till April. Passing the 'Whitewood Arena', I remembered...hockey, or specifically, ice hockey. A town with 209 people had an Ice Arena? We have five in New Zealand. Even in summer there were signs of hockey schools, hockey camps, ice rinks or arenas everywhere. They double in these towns as a meeting hall. An ice rink seems like an ironic place for locals to go warm up but that's how small town Canada works. The NHL draft was approaching and self-proclaimed expert truckers could be heard discussing hockey at every gas station. It is no surprise Canada dominates this game. Most Canadian kids can, and many do, flood their gardens for long winter seasons.

It was interesting comparing the culture to Dunedin, where I had recently taken up the game for the hell of it. A Dunedin sized city in Canada would have had a dozen ice rinks. I had absolutely enjoyed the game I had started so late in life. It involved skating! Albeit a very different kind skating from the sport that led me to this epic journey. I looked forward to playing on return.

Endless wheat fields rolled off into the horizon. As I neared the edge of the province I headed south east off Trans Canada 1 for a tiny town across the Manitoba border called Kola. In addition to what would be a record day of a whopping 390 km, I lost another hour in a time zone change. I would be arriving late. Off the main highway it grew quiet and lonely. I hadn't seen a car since I left the main highway. Having already used a few hours of battery power in the morning darkness, I delayed using front light as long as possible. It grew dark and the lights of what would be Kola seemed to take forever to arrive. With nothing to judge the distance, Kola was deceptively close.

Leon and his wife were a kind Christian family who lived in the middle of nowhere...Kola. I soaked in his hot tub while he told me about the mountain bike trails he had blazed locally. I felt a sense of security as they openly prayed for me on departure, but I was in for a miserable day.

I headed south towards the USA and as I approached the city of Brandon I hit some serious rain and direct headwind. The first signs of fatigue were starting to show. Given my navigation cockup on Day 2 there was now added pressure to get to Boston quickly and directly. It rained all day and after my second puncture of the day I threw my first serious tantrum. It was inevitable. My only choice was a hotel in a place called Killarney that would stretch the budget. Noodles and sardines for dinner. Yay!

I rolled out before sunrise, heading for the US border crossing of Sarles, separating Manitoba and North Dakota. To my relief the wind had turned. The wind was cold but when it was pushing you in the right direction it was always welcome. I arrived at the Canadian exit point 15 minutes before the border would open, having already knocked up 100 km. This was not a busy crossing point; I doubt if the customs officers would have seen a dozen cars a day. There was nobody about on either side of the large barbed wire fence.

Three friendly Canadian officials showed up and kindly offered me shelter in their office. While waiting for their American counterparts to open up the border I turned the conversation to hockey, correctly guessing that it would enhance our friendship. I was surprised how freely the Canadian officials discussed the security of the numerous crossing points on the large map on the office wall.

One hundred metres south at precisely 8:55am, two American customs officials marched out to the barrier under the star spangled banner to open the gate. The Canadian officials bade me farewell without even bothering to check my passport. I headed over the border to a booth where the US officials were preparing for the possibility of traffic that day.

The first and quite possibly the only person to enter the US at the Sarles crossing that day, I wheeled my bike toward the customs booth. "Behind the line, Sir!" barked the official, who hadn't quite finished shuffling papers at 8:59am. It would appear that Americans took security more seriously than the Canadians. Waiting patiently for the paper shuffling to end I was eventually signalled forward, and the inspection of the unusual vehicle and traveller from down under began.

The first name on the official's US customs badge read Chad and the second something much longer and Polish looking. Chad was massive and had a buzz cut. I'm sure I had seen him as a guard on an episode of 'World's Scariest Prisons'. Perhaps he'd been fired? The second official (Darlene) appeared to be Chad's superior. She would expect a great deal of diligence from Chad during my forthcoming inspection. Darlene was as wide as Chad was tall, and equally scary.

Chad and Darlene did things by the book and were a complete contrast to their friendly and casual Canadian counterparts. This unusual traveller was the perfect opportunity for Chad to practice procedures, as the stern Darlene looked on at me frowning with suspicion. After a thorough bio scan and lengthy bag check I was required to fill out a form declaring I was not a Nazi war criminal or a member of Al-Qaeda. "The processing fee is $6" demanded Chad; they would not take Canadian. "Would you accept Visa?" I was hoping to get my

US cash from the nearby town of Karlstad. "There is no Visa facility or ATM at this crossing Sir." Chad wouldn't budge, I tried to play up the importance of the record attempt and the charity for which I was riding in hope that somewhere under the thick exteriors of the border officials there was some sort of heart, sadly not. "The processing fee is $6 US" barked Darlene. "Without it you cannot enter the United States".

At a loss, my only option was looking like a 50 km back track in the hope of finding a bank back in Canada. I saw no reason why my newly made and more human Canadian friends would carry US cash, but it was worth a try so I headed 100 metres back to Canada. An official wearing a Toronto Maple Leaf hat reached into his wallet and exchanged US cash straight, not even accepting the correct exchange rate, "it's no problem buddy, have a safe trip".

Chad and Darlene seemed disappointed that I had returned so quickly and with no other traffic to deal with, decided to delay me with further interrogations, further fingerprinting and a second bike check. Eventually, concluding I wasn't working with ISIS, I was let through!! It was the one and only unfriendly encounter I would have during the entire American leg of my trip.

The patriotism of Americans was immediately

obvious with the U.S. flag proudly displayed on almost every lawn or veranda in the small prairie towns of North Dakota. The distances were now posted in miles, making progress seem less rewarding. Nonetheless I made excellent progress towards Minnesota. It was easy to lose perspective of the massive distances I was knocking out day after day. This was to be another major day. At around 4 pm, in my eyes I was nearly done. I checked with a local that I was on the right road. "You're going to Thief River Falls? By bicycle?! But you can't!!" He would never have believed I had already covered 100 km and 78 miles. With a solid tail wind I knocked up another massive day, 383 km, to the Minnesota town of Thief River Falls. My host Glen had arranged for an interview with the local media. I was tired but happy to share my story. The next day I knocked up another 300 plus through the fantastic 1000 lakes area towards Brainerd where a kind host named Susan stuffed me full of pasta.

I made steady progress through the Northern US, staying with a series of fantastic hosts through Minnesota, Wisconsin and toward Illinois. There was Jeremy, a former footballer and wrestler. Nick, an intrepid traveller and Rugby fan, Colton a young recently graduated sports journalist, all willing to offer food, shelter and encouragement. I would love to have had more time to get to know these wonderful people who all understood my need for sleep and recovery.

My legs seemed to be adapting to the daily mileage. At times I felt surprisingly sharp. Approaching Madison a large group of racing cyclists entered the road 200 metres in front of me. I kept pace and felt fine in spite of having already covered 200 km. I even started catching them. I rode up to say hi. Perhaps it was my accent, perhaps it was because I didn't resemble a racing cyclist? Perhaps it was because they were suffering, but nobody would talk to me? Someone said something nasty about my bib. I had made a habit of wearing my cycling bib over the top of my cycling jersey, this looks extremely uncool and was mocked at in a few online photos. But cool was not a priority, the bib not only served to reduce drag but helped secured the essential contents such as phone and objects in my rear pockets. I rode past the bike race and caught up with the next group who were also too cool to converse. Cyclists!

One motivator throughout the trip were the stops where I would meet old friends. Heading toward Chicago, I was looking forward to meeting John Coyle, Olympian. A silver medallist, in fact. I had competed against John in the early 1990s. John is an energetic and charismatic character who has made an excellent speaking career for himself. His motivating talks are based on the concept of time, specifically how and why it appears to speed up as we age. His reasoning: routine. John uses his energy and experience to encourage people to take risks, step out of routine and make the most of every day. I was certainly doing that. Reuniting with John and his message was a timely reminder that what I was doing wasn't mad. I was just making the most of every day. I certainly remembered every moment so far. You don't forget a race around the world by bicycle. You remember every moment.

We talked about the glory days before making an early start directly through the centre of Chicago. John knew the road, he rode without a helmet and like a bicycle courier. It was no surprise he could ride with such skill. He had after all been an Olympic medallist and an elite cyclist. I

The 'Chicago Eye' with Olympic Silver Medallist, John Coyle

I passed the eyesore industrial areas of Whiting and East Chicago on my own. The factories reminding me of the grim scenes at the end of 'The Lorax'. The Dr Seuss book where that bloody Once-ler had decimated the local surroundings. I recalled the line from the book 'I hear things are just as bad in Lake Erie'. This was a populated, polluted and unpleasant section of the US.

I stopped at a McDonald's in Gary Indiana, the ghetto suburb made famous as the childhood home of Michael Jackson. Things weren't pretty in 'the hood', with homeless people trudging alongside glum brick housing. I wondered if it really was necessary to have a 'no guns' sign on the McDonald's door until I sat down next to the bullet holes in the window beside me.

I woke after a costly hotel night in South Bend. My morning moment had become a strain, things weren't good on the stool front. Haemorrhoids had also been threatening. The morning moment was like doing a powerlifting squat. Draining and potentially race ending. I figured it was a combination of a different diet and dehydration. The days had been hot. I stopped at a pharmacy and bought some 'super lax' which seemed to have the desired effect.

I continued east and was shown extreme hospitality by several more Warm Showers hosts, who were happy to support my journey over the next few days across Indiana, Ohio and

Pennsylvania. The American people on the Warm Showers site were all truly warm and welcoming. They were supporting me and making this journey possible. I vowed to host other people when I returned home. Before departure I had rolled up a bunch of small New Zealand watercolours I'd painted. I gave them to my hosts as a token of my appreciation.

The traffic in the larger cities was becoming frustrating. The USA doesn't do roundabouts, they prefer lights. The lights are plentiful and the transitions long. Riding through Erie, Cleveland, Syracuse and Buffalo, I had several tantrums. This type of riding was killing my average speed. I would attempt to maximise efficiency by anticipating lights sometimes two or three sets in the distance. Always reminding myself that it's better to roll slowly and anticipate the green signal, than to clip out of pedals and stop. Sprinting for lights, only to have to jam on brakes when you realise the race is lost, is inefficient and dangerous.

Riding along the massive Lake Erie my background theme became Gordon Lightfoot's song, The Wreck of the Edmund Fitzgerald, 'The legend lives on from the Chippewa on down, Of the big lake they call Gitche Gumee'. I thought of Warren, remembering how it was a favourite song and agreeing that historical songs are fantastic. Edmund Fitzgerald has about 20 verses, it kept me going all day.

Despite gorging myself on massive quantities of fast food since Vancouver, I looked down at my abs one night and I was ripped! I decided to market a new weightless programme. I'd call it '3 Weeks to Toned Abs.' I would make a fancy infomercial. In only three weeks I lost eight pounds and had eaten 7000 calories per day of junk food...but that's not all!! Unfortunately, it had also taken 12 hours of cycling per day, but I didn't need to mention that. Fat loss doesn't come easy but I was losing weight already.

Day 22, I had been unable to secure a host and would have to dip into the budget, after a short and uneventful day to the rather boring town of Utica. An hour was wasted searching for anything affordable and I eventually settled for the best deal in town at the inappropriately named 'Budget Hotel'. The hotel had all the hallmarks of the hotels I would later use in Eastern Europe, only without the budget. It had the stains and stank of cigarettes. It had the unfriendly and non-English speaking proprietor, and dodgy homeless people were lingering outside. Nothing worked and sadly at the price of $80 NZ it was anything but 'budget'. Other than the endless choices of fast food, decent eating was proving costly in the US. The internet seemed to be working which was a surprise and before I began the usual online jobs I took the opportunity to sneak a look at Peter Adam Smith's progress.

I knew this was pointless. His progress, good or bad, was out of my control and Craig Lewis would have been disappointed in me. During our '94 Olympic preparation, Craig had forbidden us from even watching, let alone timing, other teams; 'Control the controllable'.

But I flicked on Peter's page, and noticed the 260 km average. He was ahead of me. I temporarily began to spiral into negative thoughts, considering the contrast of our trips. I'd wasted two hours trying to save on food and a place to sleep, yet still had yet to attend to the tiresome jobs of wrestling with my pathetic bike pump, struggling to rinse out bike shorts and endless other tasks. Peter got to flop on a comfy mattress and get a foot rub. It wasn't fair. I threw a tantrum.

I headed east, and although I never felt fully fresh, the miles kept on coming. I had consciously trained before the trip to make long rides as easy as possible, rather than as hard as possible. Speed wasn't as important as staying on the bike. This event was about looking after the body. I would deliberately ride easy. Training myself to enter a truly relaxed pedalling style. One that would just keep making use of the slow fat burning fires. In this relaxed trance like state, I rode on, keeping very much in touch with the body. By this stage I had found the optimum effort for steady movement, I'd change positions, regularly and make the effort to stretch on the bike when rolling down gentle hills. Slow and steady would win this race.

Thanks to my dad I have an intense interest in history. Getting further east my imagination floated to a different time. I'd envisaged herds of buffalo on the prairies. Now I imagined the Civil War, Illinois the land of Lincoln, the history behind the Erie Canal and the massive population growth that followed. These upper US states are associated with big cities but given the size of the continent there are still plenty of open spaces. The forest and wildlife through the Appalachian Mountains is also impressive.

Riding through the earliest areas of settlement in the original 13 colonies, and places like Williamstown and Saratoga Springs, my mind drifted to the Revolutionary War. If I had had the time I would have enjoyed stopping to study the historic signs, museums and landmarks.

My North American leg was slowly coming to its conclusion; I was still in the race, ahead of record but slightly behind Peter Smith. I was headed for Albany, New York State Capitol, where a Warm Showers host named Jim would host me. I knew I was at the right door due to the pro cycling stickers. Jim was in his '60s, and had recently ridden at a hell of pace across America. Legend! In the morning Jim led me out of Albany, I waved good bye and headed over some major climbs in the Appalachians. The first signs of fall were showing and it would soon get steadily colder.

I wasn't too far from Lake Placid New York, host of the 1980 Winter Olympics, where 35 years earlier Eric Heiden had won five Olympic Golds. I had visited Lake Placid and raced there in our disastrous 1994 campaign. The only personal best I had set on that occasion was that of being in the cold...minus 39°C. Today it was a comfortable 23 degrees.

I hit dense population as I headed south toward Hartford, where a friend of a friend named Michael was expecting me. Springfield was a navigational nightmare. There was no sign of Homer but I stopped at Tim Hortons to stuff down some donuts. Table manners had been sacrificed by this point of the journey, the combination of constant hunger and time constraints meant I ate like the Cookie Monster. My taste buds still loved the cheesy greasy fat but my immune system was about to revolt. I needed nutrients. Albany to Hartford was a big day, 300 km plus, with serious manly points.

On my last day in North America, the battle of Boston was to be fairly straight forward. Boston is a cycle friendly city with great sense of history. I headed for the centre where John Coyle had organised for a friend named Carrie to host me. During my last few hours in America I kept up rule 1. Eat! No matter what!! I didn't want to trouble Carrie for food so I stopped at what I hoped would be my final McDonald's stop in America. Poor fuel for the engine, but McDonald's restaurants were cheap and convenient. The fat and carbs served as cheap fuel, but I was starting to desperately need nutrients. Nutrients are like engine oil. If you don't top up, eventually the engine will seize.

Carrie proved to be an angel of nutrition and was a timely reminder for me to get my food right. I'm sure I'd seen her on the cover of one of those fitness magazines lying about my gym. Carrie had in fact, recently placed highly in a Miss Fitness Connecticut event. She was exactly what millions of western women aspire to be, only she hadn't got there on five minutes a day. She had got there with a disciplined and consistent exercise routine and a sound knowledge of nutrition. Carrie was a model of the American concept of fitness. Fitness pageants are at the other end of my purist views of what constitutes sport. But as an exercise consultant myself I have huge respect for those that have the discipline to compete in these events. Looking fit and athletic never comes easy.

Other than getting to the airport in the evening, I essentially had what would be a day off. Carrie kindly gave me a quick tour of Boston. I visited some of the oldest buildings in North America. Carrie also took me to 'Cheers' and shouted me a stupidly healthy meal at a Boston salad bar. I'd actually managed some sightseeing!

The remainder of the day was spent

desperately planning routes and organising potential hosts and hotels. Carrie was in the process of launching and marketing her own brand of protein bar 'Gutsey bar'! I had no doubt she would succeed, she was disciplined and motivated. Carrie had been a timely reminder of the importance of sound nutrition and gave me stacks of samples and goodies that would keep me rolling in Portugal. Thank you Carrie and God Bless America, with the exception of the border Nazis, Americans had been so good to me.

I'd made it across a very indirect route of North America and I'd averaged 250 km per day. It had taken me 24 days. It had cost me a few hundred dollars and I had met some amazing people. Even if the trip were to end here, it would have been worth it. But Leg 2 was about to start.

Chapter 9

Europe

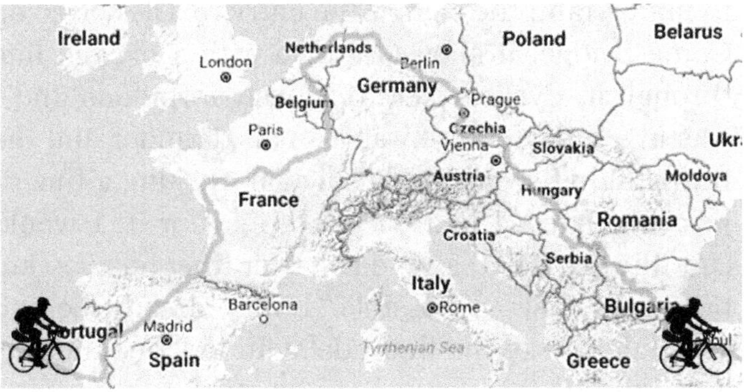

I landed at Lisbon airport having had barely four hours of plane sleep. I quickly reassembled my bike and was assured by a well-meaning tourist that the Vasco da Gama bridge across the Lisbon harbour could be crossed legally by bicycle. I headed East, making my way along a waterfront that almost reminded me of Auckland's Waitemata Harbour.

Portugal would be the first country where the language barrier would add to the challenge of the journey. Before I left I decided to write an introduction letter outlining my trip, and Google translated it into the various languages I would encounter.

'Hi My name is Andrew Nicholson from New Zealand. I'm sorry I don't speak much of your language. I am attempting a world record bicycle circumnavigation in support of cancer research' etc. etc.

Fluent Portuguese was certainly not necessary to understand the sign at the entry to The Vasco da Gama Bridge. It showed a bike with a big red line through it. Cyclists were obviously forbidden and I was in a hurry. There was a small shoulder and the traffic didn't seem overly suicidal. Risking a fine or possible arrest I had decided to go for it. I would run the gauntlet and dash over the busy 2 km bridge as fast as possible. I was already behind schedule due to the flight delay in Boston, and this was a race!!

It was the only option if I was to get to my hosts in the East of the country by dark. Pumped with adrenaline and ready to rumble, I clipped in and wound up. Seconds later I was blocked by a police car with lights fully flashing. Only two hours into my European leg and I was already in trouble!

A short and grumpy Constable Gonzales, who could have been Danny DeVito's twin, exited the vehicle, slammed his door and gestured me to vamoose back the way I had come. He was not impressed, but at least it seemed I wasn't to be arrested. I reached for my Portuguese letter but the grouch would have none of it, I was to vamoose ASAP.

I turned to backtrack down the ramp when suddenly a second police car pulled up. Everything Gonzales wasn't stepped out of the second car. Erik Estrada from 'ChiPs' strolled onto the scene with a smile, seeming more interested in my bike then the issue at hand.

By now I had now resigned to finding another way across the harbour but thought I'd try my letter on Estrada. His dark eyes lit up, he was clearly most impressed. I assumed by his interest in my bike he was a cycling fan, he said something like "Grande Vuelta", nodding approvingly.

A highly gesticulated and passionate Portuguese discussion then took place between the two officers, of which I understood nothing. The discussion became more heated and De Vito began back down and sulk.

It seemed that Estrada was the superior officer on the scene and he had sorted a solution for me. De Vito was put in his place for being unfriendly to the tourist. Arms folded and sulking, DeVito was sent back and he retreated to his patrol car, muttering and slamming the door. Estrada then enthusiastically mimed that I would be escorted across the bridge, and to follow him as fast as possible. DeVito would follow behind.

Estrada was proud and happy to help, urging me on with lights flashing. "Rapido, rapido" he shouted with thumbs up, as I was escorted at full speed to the nearest exit on the opposite side of the harbour. I waved a big thanks to the two late model patrol cars. Estrada wished me well with a return wave while DeVito and pouted gave me a hate look.

I spent some time negotiating my way out of Lisbon's hilly outer suburbs. With the plane delay it was looking like a late arrival with my pre-arranged hosts. By this stage of the journey I had become l aware of the need to keep both phone batteries fully charged. To my horror, as my phone battery faded, I realised that I had failed to charge my second battery in Boston. It was already 2 o'clock, and I'd lost my only means of navigation. I threw a tantrum and bought a road map from a gas station. I'd get there the old fashioned way.

It was a late arrival but Carrie's nutrition pack meant I didn't have to take food stops. Apart from the bridge I hadn't had to stop. My first European hosts, Eszter and Paulo, were intrepid cyclists. I apologised for my late arrival. I would later host Paulo and Eszter in my own home on their New Zealand honeymoon.

Portugal and Spain were new countries for me, as neither were seriously involved with speed skating. The inland countryside was dry and arid, with large fig and olive trees dotting the landscape. Some impressive citadels and cathedrals sat on hill tops. The country towns looked run down and relaxed, with the concept of siesta still very much part of the culture. I would have to pass on siesta, I had to cover 246 km to the city of Covilhã, where I was guided to the centre by a kind group of racing cyclists I had stumbled across. They took an interest in my letter while riding on the outskirts, guiding me to a cheap hotel.

Day 29 was to be a 300 plus day so I couldn't make the most of the included breakfast at the hotel. Breakfast didn't start till 7:00am and I needed to be on the road by 5:30am as usual. Early the next morning I crossed into Spain, pleased to discover that the price of groceries remained reasonable. Later in the day I passed through Salamanca, the first of two antipodal points I needed to pass through as per Guinness rules. Dig a hole in Salamanca and I'd come out in Kapati Coast. I was as far away from New Zealand as you could possibly get. In reality I was still far from half way but I used the benchmark as a motivator. The majority of my trip would be ridden in the Eastern Hemisphere.

A warm showers host named Paco was expecting me, in the Spanish town of Medina del Campo. Paco had arranged for a young rider named Eduardo to come out to meet me, and he mimed that he knew all about me. Cycling is huge in Spain. Paco had sent out numerous fans, and more riders from the club joined me and escorted me through the town, via the same roads where tomorrow the

8th stage of the 2015 Tour of Spain or 'Vuelta' would begin.

New Zealand professional George Bennett, an Olympian and a friend of my brother Chris, was impressively placed at the top end of GC. Crowds were gathering at the cafes in the square where the teams were being presented.

Paco's English was better than my Spanish but far from perfect. But Paco was high on energy and with typical Latin gesticulation he was easy to understand. Paco had survived two types of cancer and was proud to host me. It was touching to meet Paco, he was a reminder of the cause behind my ride and gave it some purpose. I would have loved to stayed on to see the start of the stage, but as always an early start was required.

Around mid-morning I received a message from my brother. George Bennett was apparently most impressed my ride, "Tell him to stop by at the team bus and I'll help him out", George had written to Chris. Such a shame I had picked up this message too late. I would have loved the chance to get up close with the pros and see first-hand the contrast between the care they would receive versus my day to day struggle.

George wouldn't have to ride as far as me today but he had to do it way faster. He could afford a sleep in. I had long since erased the concept of a 'sleep in', sleep could never be part of this challenge, there were just too many kilometres to cover.

In the city of Burgos I stayed with warm showers hosts Luis and Maria. I followed Luis to the local news station, passing a bullfighting arena, where an interview with the local media was arranged. I asked the Luis his opinion on the 'sport' of bullfighting. "It's barbaric" he replied, seemingly ashamed of this well-known Spanish tradition. His response didn't surprise me, having seen his peaceful interactions with his dog Booba. He and Maria had a fabulous album of their cycle trip in New Zealand; yet another couple who had really travelled. They now had a new baby but along with Booba they had no intention to stop cycle touring. Luis described the trailers he had arranged for both dog and baby. Fantastic!

For so many people, kids and pets would put cycle touring in the too hard basket but Luis and Maria had no intention of letting family life stop them. While we feasted Luis kindly connected my phone to his Wi-Fi and excitedly described the family's next cycle plans.

Before bed, I did the usual route and accommodation planning and took a quick peek at Peter Adam Smith's progress. He was out!

I momentarily felt guilty as I punched the air triumphantly. Regardless of his big budget and support, the challenges Peter had faced in China and Kazakhstan had broken him. Peter had posted a long list of reasons, justifying his withdrawal from the record attempt.

My race was far from won, but now it was only against the established record set by the official record holder, Alan Bate. The fact that I was still going gave me a huge sense of pride. It reminded me of my first season as a long track skater. I was winning a monumental challenge in spite of the lack of financial support. A big budget had proved no match for a resourceful individual and capable cyclist. I had controlled the controllable and for the most part ignored my opposition from the start.

I had a stressful day over the Pyrenees and into San Sebastián where I took a half day off to reorganise. I was amped to make it all up in one day. I knocked myself out at 7:00pm with a pill for an ultra-early start. It was raining steadily at 3:00am as I made my way into France. I'd been riding for hours in the dark and made it to Bordeaux, having already made my quota of 240 km by noon. My battery was running low, it started hosing down. I made a short backtrack to a Warm Showers host, and called it a day.

I was to spend five nights in France. My first hosts were Lydie and Pascal; Lydie had been following me daily. On previous trips to France the stereotypes of the French had proven to be true. On this trip I stayed with three awesome French families. Like the Americans, they were welcoming, friendly and doing their best to help the stranger from afar on a mission. I dispelled the French arrogance stereotype for ever. I rode through vineyards, passed castles, historic cathedrals and lots of cyclists as I rode east up the Loire valley. My progress was steady but some of the minor roads in France were deadly. Approaching Nantes I hit a gusty side wind that pushed me to the centre of the shoulder-less and narrow road. A few near misses had me shaken.

My final day in France would finish in Nancy. I stayed with a family who had just toured through South America, with their children in tow. I was meeting some real adventurers and was truly humbled.

The next day I would cover over 300 km and visit five countries. Exiting France I would cycle directly through Luxembourg, a sensible country to cycle through, taking no more than three hours from end to end. I encountered rolling hills, quaint villages and forest as I briefly entered a fantastic area of Belgium, over a large climb in the Ardennes Forest. Before heading into Holland I swooped down a long descent and briefly entered Germany. There wasn't even a sign.

Being in countries where you don't speak the language and often, they don't speak yours; brings about an uncomfortable sense of isolation, particularly for the solo traveller. But as I entered my next few countries I would feel more at home. I had a few words of the languages, having travelled extensively as a skater in this part of Europe. It was one of the reasons I chose this route. I also knew quite a few people from old skating days who had said they'd look after me for a night. I felt a particularly strong connection to Holland which had been my first experience of real travel.

In the summer holidays of 1986-87 I stacked beer crates at the Westward Ho Wholesalers in Kelston. I added my earnings to that I'd saved after school at the gas station. We did a little fundraising and with a few hundred from the club, I had just enough for an air ticket to Europe. I would join Chris and attend my first World Champs in Canada via Holland for some warm up races. I was 16 years old but I looked 11.

I travelled with Chris and another Kiwi named Phil Cavanagh. We arrived in Schiphol Airport exhausted and jetlagged from an exceptionally inconvenient flight via Fiji, Honolulu, Vancouver, Edmonton and finally Amsterdam. Despite the jetlag, my eyes were glued to the window. This was my first real experience of culture shock, it was like a movie. The old buildings, cramped houses, dense apartment blocks, canals, the sheer density of the population, hearing a different language, the tiny square patches of gardens. This was exciting! This was travel.

The skating culture in Holland was also inspirational. Speed skating is the national winter sport of the Dutch, they are passionate about it and dominate. It was speed skaters not rugby players who were endorsing products on billboards. There are artificial 400m skating tracks throughout the country. When you said you were a skater to a Dutchman, he had respect for you, he didn't ask stupid questions about Torvill and Dean.

Chris was justifiably reluctant to have me along on this trip, no doubt he felt responsible for me. He was only 19 himself and he knew I had barely a cent in my pocket. This was no organised team trip, there was no coach. Three Kiwi teenagers had simply scrounged the minimum and turned up to a world champs. After a few days, Chris and Phil left me to fend for myself at the youth hostel while they went to train and stay with friends in Belgium. I didn't have the train fare.

All manner of terrible things could have happened to me and nearly did. I got lost one afternoon on the trams in The Hague while trying to find the rink, a sea of drunk football hooligans swamped my tram and started breaking stuff. I started drawing attention so I exited the tram at the next stop. A New Zealand child was roaming around Europe with a very small handful of guilders. My Dad tried to discourage me from taking this trip but he should have simply said no! Or at least made the effort to organise billets. I was way too young and way too poor to be roaming around Europe alone.

Dutch parents and officials were baffled by how this lone Kiwi could have found his way to Europe and Canada. Why is that child racing in the worlds? He's not bad? Where the hell was his coach? Where are his parents? They took pity on me, encouraged me and offered me a place to stay if I could make it back next year. I was so grateful. Nobody in New Zealand had ever shown an interest.

The results of this first trip were average. I came dead last, at my first world championships 48th , but I was good enough to line up and I had so loved the travel! I visited several countries and this first experience gave me the travel bug that would inspire a life time of travel including my world ride.

On September 8 2015, after five countries and over 300 km, my legs were disappointed to discover that the very southern tip of Holland does actually have a few hills. A former skating fan named Gitta who would host me just happened to live at the top of the very biggest one. She lived a few kilometres outside the town of Vaals, just inside the German border. It was great to be hosted by another familiar face and be in a very familiar country. Gitta's partner Marcel worked raising funds for cancer research in Holland and took an obvious interest in my trip. As I stuffed myself on pasta

Gitta and I flicked through old skating photos and familiar faces from skating days.

The following morning, I dropped back into Belgium, along large canals, before crossing back into Holland. The population began to thicken as I approached Dordrecht, where an old friend and former Dutch skating team member Joost Smit had agreed to take care of me.

Joost's family had direct family connections with the Van der Valk Hotel chain. I arrived late to enjoy a comfortable night of luxury, all courtesy of Van der Valk Hotels. The luxury was extreme, the food was perfect and plentiful, and everything was free! I guzzled the complimentary wine as I sat in a restaurant with Joost and his former team mate Alex Velzeboer. Alex's sister had been paralysed in a skating accident in 1993. Like Mike McMillen, she had placed 4th in the 1992 Olympics. The pain of a 4th placing was no doubt small compared to that of a life in a wheelchair.

It was tough to leave the comforts of the hotel and old friends. I conducted a brief radio interview early in the morning before Joost and his friend Kurt joined me in the ride across Holland to Assen, 240 km North East. They would lead me through the rabbit warren of Holland...naar de links, naar de rechts...turn left, turn right. I went through Zwolle, known as the city of bicycles, just after school finished. Large groups of helmetless students rode along the cycle paths on basic machines, chatting each other up, on their way home. A perfect reminder of how the bicycle is such a fantastic and practical form of transport in this flat and densely populated country.

After a meal at the Van der Valk Hotel in Assen, Joost and Kurt headed back home by train. Joost had been a welcome relief from the isolation, and like John Coyle or Mike Bentley, it was great to reunite with friends from the past.

I entered Germany and endured a couple of rainy days and a series of navigation and puncture stresses. Joost had arranged yet another night of comfort at the historic town of Hildesheim. Spoilt with more luxury, I calmed down somewhat before heading south towards Eastern Europe.

In Halle (Saale), Germany, I stayed with the friend of an Australian speed skater who lived near the centre. Christoph was clearly expecting me, calling out from the third story of a glum looking apartment block. He was cherry, super helpful and had been a keen follower of my trip. He lived in student accommodation in a tiny flat along with several interesting international students, who happily made room for me. It was Friday night and I had to decline their offer to 'come and meet some friends' for an hour.

These types of hours usually end up becoming five. Under normal circumstances I would love to have chatted with these motivated and energetic young Europeans, but I had logistics and bike duties to attend to. Christoph understood and we chatted while I ate the mammoth portion of student spaghetti he presented to me.

As I caught up on all the flat tubes and tire pumping. I started ranting to Christoph about my pump, grizzling about the old days and the need for a good old fashioned thruster pump. "Oh, like this? I bought it for five Euros?" said Christoph. My pumping muscles were envious and immediately asked if I could test it. Within half a dozen thrusts I had plenty of pressure in my tyres. I begged to buy it from him but he kindly donated it. Wanting to keep weight to a minimum I left him my $50 mini. I know I got the better deal. Basics is so often better than fancy. Christoph headed out and left me to it, every moment was precious. Chains needed wiping and oiling, food needed to be bought and readied for the bike. Lights attached, batteries constantly charged or replaced.

Given the organising required not a moment could be wasted. A 4:30am start means rising at 4:15am. I needed to be ready to go, to be able to wake up and simply step on the bike. Everything had to be prepared the night before. I was getting less sleep than I'd ever had in my life, at a time when needed it most, but I was coping. I still made sure I got a minimum of six hours. With help of zopiclone I was out instantly every night. Any less would have broken me. Sleep is the best form of recovery.

I hadn't expected to see Christoph again but bumped into him at 4:15 am the next morning. He was going to bed just as I was leaving. I was glad I declined his offer of the student party. I was on my bike by 4:30 am, having had a reasonable sleep. I had a 340 km planned to my in-laws in Prague and there would be both hills and traffic.

The 'morning moment', which often became first available public toilet or gas station, was no time to be dwelling. I'd whip out Google Maps to get my daily bearings and check the daily route. A valuable few moments that could be used for route finding. On this trip there wasn't even time to enjoy a morning dump.

With so many kilometres required an early start was essential. You beat heat, traffic, wind and set yourself up with a good buffer before inevitable dramas unfold. Once on the bike I enjoyed the stupidly early starts. Starting early gave me a good sense of security, knowing I had all day to reach my goal. At times I could have covered 100 km by 7:30am, it gave me the confidence to get through the rest of the day.

Beyond Dresden I headed up a huge climb and into the east across the Czech border. Things beyond what was once the Iron Curtain become instantly less kept. Graffiti increased as did rubbish and the standard of driving became significantly more wild. I still felt at home. I knew the Czech Republic through Marcela, having spent a few months here five years earlier. I even had a few words of the language to keep me from feeling like a complete idiot.

I swept down of the into medieval towns of Teplice, Ústí nad Labem, along the Elbe River and then the Vltava. I knew the way having ridden out this way from Prague five years earlier. I was excited about seeing my in-laws. I'd been dreaming of the dumplings and large portions of Czech dishes that my mother-in-law had waiting. The Czech Republic wasn't all Stalin worship, cabbage soup and boiled potatoes.

I had barely hours to spend with my truly lovely in-laws. Marcela's parents spoke no English so my limited Czech becomes the common language. This still makes for a halted conversation because my Czech is a combination Dutch, German and Norwegian with occasional Czech words thrown in, most of those names of food. I was on the other side of the world in the centre of this busy but beautiful medieval city but I suddenly felt I was home.

My in-laws are a model family of fun and closeness. They are the sum of my amazing wife who had selflessly let me take on this epic four month challenge. I wanted a break and I knew it would be hard to leave my family. We laughed, Mumka stuffed me with knedlíky (Czech dumplings) and Gabi (my sister in law) and Borek attended to all my bicycle and body needs. I was in a hurry to make up the kilometres but needed more time with them, I didn't want to ride tomorrow. I woke in a comfortable and familiar bed and used the valuable time on Gabi's laptop to book tickets to India and beyond. Behind schedule, I still needed to peg back the daily average, but I opted for a short day to the family weekend house in Southern Bohemia setting off through the centre of Prague Vecheslav's Square. I cycled past the tourist sites, the Charles Bridge and past numerous tourist groups following their allocated banner.

The whanau would follow me and I had support for the very short day, 113 km to the weekend house near the city of Pisek. What a contrast this trip was to my previous Czech visit. I had done an ESOL (English as a Second Language) certificate in Prague five years ago. I would spend warm, relaxing weekend breaks in the same southern Bohemian countryside. Marcela and I would go for 30 - 50 km cycling jaunts to visit the medieval castles in the local area.

The demands of this epic race were so very different. I slept in my in-law's family bach in the village of Zlivice on the Otava River, missing Marcela terribly. I was woken by my Czech support team at 5:00am. They followed me for the first few hours before it was time to part, approaching eastern Czech Republic. It was an emotional parting and I bawled like a baby.

A sad farewell with extended family in the Czech Republic

Seeing my Czech family had made me miss Marcela. I knew the tough stuff hadn't even started. From here on the countries would get lonely, and at times unfriendly. I would have nothing of the languages. No more old friends to look forward to until Perth, and lots of unknowns between. I wasn't even half way and I was barely in touch with the record. It was a hilly, windy and lonely day to Brno with some nasty traffic adding to the pressure.

I stayed overnight with Lenka, a friend of Gabi, and headed south the next day, spending a few hours in Slovakia which seemed fractionally more Eastern than the Czech Republic.

I was successful in the battle of Bratislava. The capital of Slovakia lacks the medieval feel of central

Prague, it felt surprisingly modern and a series of straight boulevards led me directly south over the Danube River. I really missed Marcela along this road, where I had memories of our previous visit, passing the same stretch of forest where Marcela and I had freedom camped. I got my first puncture for the day, the tantrum was mild thanks to Christoph's pump.

My third country for the day was to be Hungary, 20 km from the Slovakian border. I called it a day in the rather dull looking and sounding city of Győr. I had booked in at the Mukanzi Panzió hotel, the cheapest I could find online at $47 NZ. The grumpy proprietor gave me a hate look for interrupting his football game. He threw a key at me and I got what I paid for at this place. Nothing worked, including the heater, just as the nights were getting colder. I carried out the usual maintenance tasks and hooked into my supermarket stash, including a $3 bottle of wine and hit the sack. I had a big day planned.

Hotels were just places of shelter. No matter what star, all I had to do was prepare, eat and sleep. One star would do fine. There was little incentive to hang around Győr. I needed to cross Hungary in a day; 320 km.

After a frosty start, the sun came up as I rode over a cone shaped hill past the Benedictine or Territorial Abbey of Pannonhalma. This impressive medieval building is one of the oldest historical monuments in Hungary. Founded in 996 it was seriously old and way more interesting than Győr. Swooping down the hill I soon re-joined the main 81 road south, encountering increasingly heavy traffic .

The traffic seemed to be thicker than it was five years earlier and I became unsure about the legality of riding on this single lane road. There were confusing signs with ambiguous pictures of cyclists. I couldn't determine whether they were warning motorists to watch out for cyclists, or that cyclists were forbidden. I couldn't understand a word of the text. I don't think Hungarian is really a written language, just random letters thrown together, Z,K and V are popular. Hungarian Scrabble must be impossible.

After a few near swipes from behind I assumed the words 'nem kerékpározás' actually meant 'watch for cyclists' as I certainly wasn't being given much space. Opting for an annoying and indirect route, I soon found a safer road leading to the unpronounceable city of Székesfehérvár, where I gorged myself on a calorie dense Hungarian staple called Lángos. Greasy soft dough with stacks of sour cream, cheese and garlic. I had four. These pastry delights are the Kiwi equivalent of a pie, they were cheap and I scoffed them at roadside stalls all day, trying in vain to negate the usual daily calorie deficit.

Unlike its neighbours it seems cycling is not

part of Hungarian culture? There are virtually no cyclists. By now I was convinced that the confusing signs were saying 'try and kill cyclists'. The last 80 km to Szeged, I opted for another indirect secondary road. This road had a uniquely annoying surface. The surface was smooth but the levelling was appalling and consistently inconsistent. It was impossible to settle, it was not heavy chip, just wavering random undulating shakes. I was being thrown about like a rag doll. I threw a tantrum. Riding on the aero bars was not safe.

I began to spot the first of Gypsy types and the occasional use of horse or donkey carts. I was getting East.

I would arrive in Szeged in the dark. Donát would host me that night; a friendly Police Detective who lived in a tidy house in the centre. Another fantastic stranger from a faraway land.

Just after sunrise I crossed into Serbia where Syrian refugees were waiting at the border. Hungary had recently increased security on its southern borders in an attempt to stem the flow from the Syrian refugee crises. I appeared to be the only one heading out of Hungary and spent a warm afternoon riding through corn fields heading South towards Belgrade. The Cyrillic script took time to decipher. Next morning, I bypassed Belgrade and entered the same stretch of the Danube Gorge Marcela and I had cycled along, five years earlier. I took a rare break at The Golubac Fortress.

The large intimidating castle is strategically placed at the narrowing entrance of the Danube Gorge. The castle clearly guards the main waterway of Eastern Europe. Built early in the 14th century, it has changed hands between Turks, Serbs, Bulgarians and Hungarians; and Turks again.[4] An obvious place for death and violence. Clearly whoever controlled this bit of the Danube, controlled Eastern Europe.

The Danube Gorge is like the Manawatu Gorge only enlarged by 300 percent, with a few massive bluffs to climb along the edges. The river serves as the natural border of Serbia and Romania. The traffic was thinning, fewer people in this part of the world can afford private transport. As the sun went down I crossed the Danube for a fourth time and entered the 15th country on my trip, Romania. Things instantly appeared poorer again, as did the increase in horse and donkey traffic.

I recognised another experience that had contributed to my belief that breaking this record was possible. I had scouted ahead. I never ever thought I'd come this way again but my prior experience was yet again proving a valuable asset in my record attempt. Knowing the way and what to expect certainly helped.

I crossed the Danube for the fifth and final time, into Bulgaria and on a newly built modern highway. I would stop at Vidin just off the main road. I went past the Baba Vida Castle built in 1222 that Marcela and I had visited together, five years earlier. There would no tourist stops today, my stop would be brief. I needed to obtain Bulgarian cash, food and keep moving. I had made a good start in spite of the border delay and was eager to knock out 300 km toward the centre of the country.

The first ATM I stopped at had been the victim of a failed smash and grab raid. It wasn't dispensing anything. The second told me that my transaction could not be completed, as did the third. Panic set in - I still needed cash. I had no Bulgarian money and needed to get moving. The credit card wouldn't work. I managed to get a message to Jennie to see if she could top up another card. I couldn't risk riding on without sufficient cash. I found a cash exchange and got rid of several types of extra currency I had accumulated. I needed every cent I could get. Before I left Marcela also threw in a variety of leftover banknotes from previous trips. Hungarian forint, Czech koruna, euros. The cash exchange happily took it all at exorbitant rates, with the exception of the Tongan pa'anga. The cashier laughed when I tried to change it. She had never heard of Tonga.

I had no idea how long the cash crisis would last. There were several beggars hanging around. I felt guilty shooing them away but I needed every cent I could get. I really must have been the only tourist to have ever visited places like this twice. I didn't want to continue without assurance that I had currency. Frustrated, I accepted the delay, and called it a day. I spent the afternoon trying to get Chris to plan and monitor my route ahead.

I awoke at 4.30am, checked a machine and realised I could withdraw cash!! Jennie had pulled magic strings, and I was off. The outskirts of Vidin were depressing. Decrepit, abandoned warehouses lay scattered everywhere. Grey is popular, the street pavement is broken, giving the whole city a kind of permanent 'unfinished and abandoned' feel. Factories, which look like they closed with the downfall of communism in 1990, made for an ugly eyesore. Employment was clearly hard to come by. Even at 5:00am scantily clad 'working' girls lined the highway east, offering up their services to passing truckers. Food had become drab, Eastern Europe isn't known for its variety of exquisite dishes. Most of the dishes are a combination of three ingredients: bread, potatoes and meat. People here have good reason for depression but they just seem to get on with things.

Before I chose to take on this journey, there was little doubt that I was depressed, given my unemployment and financial situation. My sports career was long over and in spite of my qualifications and experience I had nothing to get up for. But I didn't need to see someone. I refused to be the person who played the depression card, despite having every reason to do so. Call me a heartless old-school bastard, but I still believe that in many cases depression is a weakness, not an illness. You do need to get on with life, no matter what has been served up. Certainly the case in less fortunate countries, like Bulgaria.

The TV advertisements such as those fronted by former All Black John Kirwan are an attempt to address the issue of depression in New Zealand. I understand that depression affects people in different ways, but are we perhaps simply creating a bunch of whiners? Being depressed has become more than acceptable, it seems to have become almost fashionable. I question whether it has become a crutch for people, in some cases a means to get attention, an excuse to stop trying? When John Kirwan decided he was depressed, he at least had fame, fortune, respect, and opportunity. I had none of that, but then I was probably tougher than John Kirwan. Perhaps John Kirwan really did need to 'harden up'. Why should our society afford the health care costs to counsel and medicate every person claiming to feel 'unfulfilled'? No such service exists for those in third world countries where people really do have good reason for depression.

I knew why I was depressed. I had every reason to complain but I knew what I had to do. Something, anything. Talking to someone may have let me express my feelings, a pill may have made me feel better, but neither would have got me a job or changed my circumstances. Sitting on the couch moping certainly wasn't going to make me feel any better. If I wasn't going to land a job I still needed to do something with my time. In my case I had chosen to race around the planet by bicycle.

Cycling in Bulgaria was becoming extremely dangerous. The lack of safe infrastructure, and a mixture of late model and old model cars on the country's highways, contribute to a high fatality rate for road accidents. The stretch between Lovech and the Troyan turn off was particularly nasty. As with Hungary, things appeared to have gotten worse since I cycled along the same road five years earlier. The were no passing lanes and plenty of blind corners. The driving habits were fast and aggressive.

This west to east road through the centre of the country connects the cities of Sofia and Varna. It is busy and lethal for any means of transport. There was virtually no shoulder and strings of traffic were approaching from both directions. It seemed an accident (preferably not involving me) was inevitable during this sector.

I was relatively safe as long as I kept hopping onto the gravel shoulder. If I used the 'right to space' 1.5-metre buffer motorists are supposed to apply in New Zealand I would have been killed within minutes. After 40 km of hopping back and forth between the road and shoulder, traffic around me started to slow. A queue of cars began to form and the traffic came to a stop. I plodded through the stationary traffic and headed toward the front of the jam. Sure enough, one car lay upside down and a terrifying sound of pain was coming from the mangled wreck of the other. As a cyclist I was able to discreetly move past the grisly scene of onlookers and those assisting with the tragedy. There was nothing I could do.

With traffic now blocked behind me, other than an ambulance heading down toward me I enjoyed a stress free finish to the day. I had the lane to myself. One person's rush to save five seconds had delayed thousands of motorists by hours, and changed others' lives forever. The obvious cause was speed.

I ignored aggressive drivers in Bulgaria rather than responding in anger, reminding myself that the drivers of such vehicles may be driven by armed and organized crime figures. In some cities, late at night, the traffic lights blink yellow in all directions which leaves rights-of-way unclear and contributes to frequent accidents. Roads are madness in Bulgaria.

After nearly 300 km I arrived at the mountain town of Troyan, which sits at the foot of the 1700m Troyan Pass. After stocking up for another big day I gorged myself on pasta and vodka. The next day started at the super early time of 4:00am and I set about tackling the two hour climb over the Balkan Mountains in the dark. I was pleasantly surprised to discover that EU funding had afforded road improvements since my previous visit. I had a stunning view as the sun rose on the summit. Europe lay behind me and the massive continent of Asia was in the East. I made excellent progress for the rest of the day and had torn across Bulgaria in two days, covering nearly 600 km. I was still in touch with the record. I had made up for the cash crisis delay with solid dawn till dusk riding, and was about to enter Asia. I called it a day at the town of Svilengrad on the Turkish border.

Chapter 10

The East

In the 5:00am darkness my navigation was telling porkies. I could see the main highway to Turkey a couple of hundred metres away on my right, but the joining road that Google Maps insisted was, wasn't. I threw a tantrum and ended up climbing a fence and trudging through a muddy ditch to walk to the highway. Being covered in thick mud would look bad at the border. I washed the worst of it off in a fresh rain puddle and dug the mud out of my cycling cleats.

I knew to ready my New Zealand Passport. I'd

crossed the same border with Marcela five years earlier and had attempted entry on my UK passport. I received a grumpy reception from the customs officer, who demanded 20 Euro for a visa. Wanting to avoid the fee I had tried my New Zealand Passport. 'Anzac', New Zealand? His mood changed and he immediately stamped my Kiwi passport. "You are my bruders" he said, pointing me towards the Gallipoli Peninsular 200 km south.

Australians and New Zealanders get an automatic visa to enter Turkey. The First World War and the madness of the Gallipoli Campaign down the road is as much a part of the Turk's history as it is Kiwis and Aussies. The connection of the event has extended to international relations 100 years on.

Stupidly I went to the first of the road side exchanges I could find and later discovered that I had been thoroughly ripped off. I hadn't had time to do my homework on the exchange rates and fortunately had exchanged only a handful of Bulgarian Lev. I received about half of what I should have. A coin operated water blaster at a petrol station in Edirne proved helpful for removing the remainder of the morning's Bulgarian mud. Apart from the chain, my bike hadn't been cleaned since Joost's mechanic did it back in Holland as there simply hadn't been time. I didn't care how my bike looked. I kept the chain clean and lubed, I put air in the tires and hoped it would keep going. I turned directly south for the Gallipoli

Peninsula. The call to prayer became a familiar sound as did the sights of people bustling off to the many modern looking mosques. I was getting closer to Asia.

By three o'clock I came to the top of a long climb. Amongst the dry scrub and pine forest, 40 kilometres in the bay to the west, was Anzac Cove. Exactly 100 years earlier, tens of thousands of Allied troops were attempting to invade Turkey for both king and country. On my previous visit, Marcela and I had spent three days at a beautiful campsite two km from Anzac Cove. In the summer warmth we spent our time in sombre thought, as we roamed around silent amongst the endless graves of those who lived in less fortunate times.

On October 7th 2015 I arrived in the seaside town of Gelibolu (Gallipoli) for a second time. I had done my quota of kilometres, a fairly standard 240 km, from Bulgaria. I was trashed but I'd become used to that. My Warm Showers host for the night was a friendly and very Turkish looking Gurol. He spoke excellent English and had served in the Turkish military. He was a keen mountain biker, a novelty sport in Turkey. Gurol laughed at the Turkish letter I had translated via Google and set about getting it to make sense. I stayed at his friend Ozbek's apartment overlooking the busy Dardanelles Straits that separate Europe and Asia. I was glad I could spare an hour to go to town for tea and a meal with Gurol. He had numerous questions about western values, politics and religion. I gave him my opinion but in my fatigued state my opinion was probably impaired. Poor Turkey, stuck in the middle of the world, so close to so much strife and change.

The following morning, I took the first of the ferries across the narrow Dardanelles Strait, setting off in pleasant sunshine along the south coast of the Sea of Marmara. My goal for the day was the city of Bursa. The double divided highway east had a smooth tarmac surface and wide shoulder. Riding conditions were comfortable but there was certainly more traffic than I had anticipated. I had a slight headwind but with so much traffic push it felt like a tailwind. I was now hooking into Asia and still in the game. Cultures and faces were changing and I understood nothing of the language.

I'd been in Turkey for two days now and had learned three Turkish words: *'Teşekkür ederim'*, thank you; *'rakim'*, altitude; and *'nufus'*, population. Approaching towns, signs were posted showing the 'rakim' and 'nufus'. For a racing cyclist these were bad words. They usually meant hilly and dangerous. Avoiding rakim and nufus would prove difficult in Turkey.

I approached Bursa and the traffic condensed and squeezed. The city was represented by quite a big but not the biggest of dots on Google Maps. Figuring a population of a manageable 300,000, I entered the city assuming that the bloke who painted the nufus sign had made a mistake. But it was me who made the mistake. Bursa is massive! 3,000,000! Three million! Most of the population of New Zealand, in a city I am embarrassed to say I'd barely heard of. My brothers would have had me beaten if I'd showed such ignorance in a family geography quiz.

Bursa couldn't be avoided without going over massive mountains. Geographical study and detailed route planning was another of the jobs that I had run out of time for. By this stage I was just getting up and riding the most obvious road east. Riding east and surviving one day at a time. The battle of Bursa was about to begin.

Although dwarfed by Istanbul, which I had the sense to avoid, Bursa certainly needed a bigger dot on Google Maps. There were no bicycles on the road, just fast and aggressive traffic. A major hazard is pedestrians who burst out in all directions from the numerous minibuses which would constantly be leapfrogging me. People explosions would begin well before the buses would come to a standstill. The same buses would zip ahead dozens of times with a never ending explosion of new people. It was getting dangerous and with evening rush hour approaching I needed more time to adjust to this surprisingly busy and modern city. I stopped on its western edge after 236 km. I would finish Bursa tomorrow morning.

I spotted an 'Otel' sign and a smiling hotel owner beckoned me over. My vocab wasn't getting me a hotel room so I turned to Gurol's newly translated letter. Within a minute the manager summoned his equally friendly staff members over and he read aloud my intro letter. Phones were whipped out and photos were taken with this most interesting and rare type of visitor. The manager then waved me to speak on the phone.

"Err, hello, this is Andrew?" I said down the line, not knowing who to expect at the other end of the line. (Familiar Australian accent) *"er...hello, this is Andrew?"* "Andrew? from Australia?" *"Yes, how can I help?"* The helpful Australian Andrew was living and working in Turkey. He knew the manager, a nice friendly mate of his. The staff continued to discuss my trip, study my bike and tried to make me as comfortable as possible.

Through Andrew I was told that if there was anything I needed the manager would oblige. The hotel even gave me a discount. Pretty cool! I'd just been led to believe by many that all middle eastern people were terrorists. Meeting such friendly staff was a reminder to withhold stereotypes. I doubt if we ever meet a big enough sample of people to make accurate character judgements of other groups. There are good and bad people everywhere.

I stocked up at a convenient supermarket, and poured large amounts of yoghurt inside me while fixing punctures and watching Beavis and Butthead on tele. I saw the Turkish word for "fartknocker" in the subtitles but forgot to write it down.

I was on the bike by 5:00am and spent an hour fighting traffic on the way out of this massive city. Rush hour starts straight after Prayer One and by 5:30am the population was already on the move. Life in Bursa is busy, people here clearly have to work harder for basics, they seem to fit more in their days than Kiwis. There is a greater sense of urgency. More needs to be done for baseline survival. People in Turkey were doing okay, they just looked busy.

Not long out of Bursa, I hit the first big Turkish hills. I was expecting this but with a decent surface and some traffic push I made good time towards Eskişehir. This city had a more manageable 'nufus' of only around a million.

The modern buildings and roads in these cities lacked the ancient feel of the poky streets of old Istanbul. Large regimental apartments dotted the hillsides, littering was popular. The cities were dense, Turkey is moving ahead fast.

I still needed a big day and after 200 km I decided to push beyond Eskişehir for a smaller dot on the map called Sivrihisar, another 100 km east. There was nothing between the two so I was committed. I pushed on over an arid and empty plain.

Before departure people would asked me if I was nervous. The answer was generally no. There was no need for nerves. I would control the controllable, and I was the right man for the job. But, inevitably, imaginary nightmare scenarios did occasionally enter my thoughts. One such occurring vision had me lost in the wilds of Turkey. I'd be shivering in my bivvy bag with packs of hungry dogs prowling outside.

The traffic thinned out and it was getting both cold and dark quickly. I was heading towards a Turkish winter. The highway grew eerily quiet and I switched on my lights. Already in my maximum warmth clothing, I went foraging through the roadside litter and picked up a discarded Turkish newspaper. I shoved the paper down my top for its intended purpose, insulation. Bear Grylls would have been proud. Now out of Europe, the sense of isolation was really starting to grow. Things were getting spooky.

Dogs became a concern. The last thing I needed was a mangy mutt sinking its teeth into my leg. Forget the initial blood loss. With the danger of infection or disease I would have needed to seek medical attention as soon as possible. The race would be have been over. Rabies would be a huge concern, especially in less developed parts of the world.

Earlier that morning I'd outpaced a couple of dog attacks. The dogs were small and their efforts half-hearted. Nonetheless it was a sign to install my DPS (Dog Prevention System). I was anticipating bigger and more motivated canines. The DPS consisted of a wieldable stick bungeed under the aerobars, and a couple of sizeable stones tucked under my bike shorts readied for good measure. I'd read lots of horror stories in cycle touring blogs about the evil dogs from Eastern Turkey. I needed to be ready.

Dog dazers are indeed effective tools against angry dogs. Marcela and I had used one before, but avoiding the extra bulk I had arranged to pick mine up in Holland from a parcel forwarded to Joost. The parcel never arrived in time; along with some bike parts it never got to me. Marcela and Joost tried to forward it along the way but I kept outrunning it. I would have to defend myself against dogs the caveman way. Sticks and stones.

It was only a matter of time and sure enough, growling on my right, a snarling beast angled towards me in the darkness! We gathered speed, the dog was big and highly pissed off! Panicking as expected, I growled and screamed in return like a madman, I hurled the rocks and reached for my weapon. With the help of a gradual downhill, Fang was eventually dropped and I had successfully fended off my first night time attack. My heart was racing; the worry dial moved up a notch. Stay calm with dogs they say? Yeah right!

As it grew colder I still couldn't see any sign of

Sivrihisar and started to hear howling. I would have expected to have seen lights by now. My dog nightmare was becoming a possible reality. The only difference was that I'd be without my bivvy bag. I dumped it in Canada long ago. Their dinner would be served unwrapped.

Eventually the lights of Sivrihisar appeared but they were few and far between. I wouldn't get eaten by wolves tonight, but I wasn't entirely sure I would find a place to sleep. Unlike Bursa, this place deserved a much smaller Google Map dot. Fortunately, I easily found the one hotel where an officious receptionist took four months to fill out the totally unnecessary forms. A kebab shop and store of sorts was also thankfully still open. I stuffed myself with kebabs, two litres of yoghurt and set about jobs for Day 59. Beavis and Butthead was on again ...YES!!

I awoke to frost and stuffed my cycling gear with a Turkish real estate magazine. The plan was to head north for a bit and then south of Ankara I would manly onwards, east as usual. It was best to avoid cities. The only reason for visiting cities was friends, family and accommodation. Avoiding them completely was difficult. I'd already been through some whoppers; Cleveland, Boston, Prague, Chicago.

I stopped for food at the intersection and with net coverage received an urgent message from mission control. This Amazing Race competitor had been given a road block. My Indian visa was not in order. I would need to get to the Indian Embassy in Ankara by 4pm.

The 'Instagram model twins' I had seen in the recent TV series 'The Amazing Race' had had it easy. I wasn't permitted to flag down a taxi. I wouldn't get to do my make up in an air-conditioned cab or play ugly tourist for the camera. I certainly wasn't going to get a million dollars if I got there on time. Naturally the embassy was directly in the centre of Ankara.

I went into race mode!! I wasn't going to quit. The race had already thrown a huge amount of rubbish at me but no way would I quit! I would do my best! I pushed harder and I took risks. The traffic intensified, two lanes each direction grew to four as I saw the massive 8 million nufus sign. As expected, Ankara was huge and thick with pollution! Thousands of identical apartment blocks covered the surrounding hills. Caught up in traffic flow, sprinting for lights and aided by a tailwind I made surprisingly rapid progress. Bicycles had not been a feature on these roads so I went as fast as the cars and somehow got away with it. The intensity of the ride into Ankara had me exhausted. I made it to the Indian Embassy 30 minutes before closing time.

The pompous embassy official deliberately made things difficult, but it looked like things would be sorted. I had raced into Ankara at full speed and had done my best to resubmit my visa application. I would learn the outcome of the visa in the morning. If the visa was sorted, I'd continue, if not; Te Aho World Ride would end. If that happened, I would head to the Ankara Train Station, see some sights, and go home.

When I woke on 10 October, my E Visa for India had been granted. I would not be packing my bike and I was not eliminated from the race. I stuck around for the included breakfast, hoping for morning traffic to subside. When it didn't, I headed North East toward Çankırı. As I was heading towards the outer suburbs, a series of ambulances and police vehicles were heading in the opposite direction at full speed with sirens wailing. Something major had just happened.

At 10:04am local time, two bombs were detonated outside Ankara Central Railway Station. The death toll was 103 civilians, and more than 500 people were injured. The attack was the deadliest terror attack in modern Turkish history.[5] I later wondered, where I might have been, had my visa not been issued?

The traffic thinned as I turned north to the small city of Çankırı. The road deteriorated and I encountered the first of the climbs Chris had warned me about. The intensity of the calls to prayer increased as did the stares. By now the faces definitely had a more middle eastern look. I pedalled through dry and arid valleys surrounded by grazing animals and large rolling hills. In Çankırı, I checked into a seriously dodgy looking hotel. I knew I was getting east, squat toilets and absence of toilet paper had become the norm.

On my evening food forage, I began feeling self-conscious in my sports shorts. I needed a decent pair of long pants, but finding a pair would just be another job, cost more money, and add another item to lug around the world.

Leaving Çankırı at dawn I immediately began a category 1 climb. Chris had been trying to give me profiles of the approaching days and generally he got it right. On Day 61 either he had screwed up or the mapometre had lied to him. He said something like, "It shouldn't be too hilly, considering it's Turkey". The second climb went on for close to two hours, I had a tantrum and blamed Chris. I rode through a large ski area and over a pass with a rakim of a whopping 1800 metres. Roadworks on the downward side also made progress slow as I dropped down into the city of Kastamonu. A third climb out of the city was as long as the last. As I approached the coast it was getting greener, with stunning views over large pine forests.

After two more Category 1 climbs, an endless series of switchbacks and several more hours of grovelling, I finally looked down over the black sea.

Equally black clouds were building in the distance. The day to Inebolu had been the equivalent of a tough mountain stage in the Tour de France. Minus any help and having to lug my own stuff. I'd been riding like this now for two months, day in day out.

The suffering had only partly been negated by the amazing scenery. It was the best since the Rockies. It started raining and it was brakes on all way down a heavily chipped 1000m descent to the coastal town of Inebolu. I was spent. After only 210 km I achieved a personal worst average of 24 kph. I found a basic hotel, maintained mind, body and bike; and fell asleep.

I woke to rain, and feeling drained I began plodding along the very neglected coastal road east. The surface was terrible, I was being bounced around dangerously on the numerous steep and slippery descents. These hills weren't like the massive passes I went over the previous day, but they were endless. I must have hauled myself over 30 coastal bluffs. My personal worst average improved to a pitiful 22 kph. By late afternoon I had struggled to the coastal city of Sinop.

In 1852 the entire Turkish fleet was destroyed here by the Russians in the early part of the Crimean war.[6] It was the first naval battle in which exploding artillery shells were used, and the Turkish fleet was annihilated. I imagined this very one sided battle and other ancient events that took place on this historic piece of coastline, right back to Jason and the Argonauts, and the ancient Hittites, through to the Greeks and the Ottoman Empire. Turkey has 3500 years of civilisation. On a trip with Marcela we would have stopped to visit the museum and fortress, soak up the history, followed perhaps by a stroll through the ancient centre of this popular tourist spot. Not on this trip, I just continued suffering.

The wind still savagely blew against me but at least the broken chip and hills came to an end as I joined the D5, a modern well sealed and busy highway that would lead all the way to Georgia. I rode the final 30 km to Gerze, another historic port, and negotiated an affordable hotel in German. My limited German was sometimes an asset in Turkey, with many Turks having links to those living in Germany.

My hair was turning into a mop and I shaved it bald in celebration of having passed the halfway point. I looked like Kojak but skinnier. My bike computer read 14,521 km. I had passed halfway. Was I enjoying it? Perhaps, at times, but no matter what happened from here on in, I had made a good go of it. It was still a matter of one day at a time.

The following morning, I found a pastry substance and set off thankfully with a slight tailwind. It looked gloomy and started to rain. Recently built apartment blocks of the standard design were continuing to populate this busy piece of coastline. Modern Turkey was orderly looking but the rubbish continued to be an eyesore.

On the D5 I encountered the first of what would be dozens of modern tunnels. The government had anticipated progress along this section of the coast and the engineering of this new highway was impressive. With numerous steep valleys running sharply to the coast, the only way to put in a serious coastal road was by blowing holes in the mountains. For 800 km, all the way to Georgia, ran dozens of these twin tunnels. Two lanes in each direction, made for motor traffic and heavy transport of which there was plenty. There was no indication that cyclists were forbidden but I still hadn't seen a single racing cyclist in Turkey yet. The Turkish authorities probably assumed that nobody would be stupid enough to try.

The first tunnel I encountered was a relatively short 800m long. The date of construction and length of each tunnel was posted at the entry points. 800 metres; I scanned behind me, hoping to run the gauntlet before the distant traffic could catch me in the narrow darkness. A serious extended sprint would do it, I switched on my lights and wound up speed.

The danger was immediately obvious, with the disappearance of the normally ample shoulder. Once in the tunnel, only a few centimetres lay between the greasy line of the road edge, to where a raised curb stepped up a full 300mm to the emergency walkway. Forced to ride in the far right of the slippery right hand lane, the sound of a truck approaching from behind amplified towards me, and the advancing noise was truly terrifying. A blasting horn added to the terror and the roar of engine built and built as the monster chased me down in the damp and greasy tube.

My sprint was getting weaker as I desperately tried to reach salvation, the literal light at the end of the tunnel. The exit grew closer as did death from behind. Seconds after my victorious exit, an enormous truck thundered past within inches of me, my whole bike buffeting around dangerously in the following wind rush.

The options for getting safely through the tunnels of doom were limited. Carefully picking gaps in the traffic, I managed a couple of narrow wins on some shorter tunnels, but I soon approached a 3 km whopper. Continuing on the road was suicide and there were no alternative routes. The emergency walkway was barely wide enough to ride on but it was the only safe way through. Made from a row of narrow rectangular concrete slabs, it was rideable with extreme care. I plodded along the narrow side walk cautiously in the dark at no more than jogging speed. Occasionally a slab of concrete would be missing. If I'd failed to spot it, I would have dropped into the Turkish sewage system. It was painfully slow going. I was relatively safe up on the walkway but extreme care had to be taken to stay on the jarring path, not fall into traffic or down drains. Such fun.

I woke to a third day of thick heavy rain in Fatsa. Neither the hotel fan or heater had worked and my struggles to get my spare clothes dry had been for nothing. The rivers on my right were swollen to capacity. I thought of the West Coast of New Zealand in spring. Greymouth would have been proud, the rain just wasn't stopping.

On top of my rain jacket I decided to start the day out with a poncho. Using trusty duct tape, I would hook the forward cover of the poncho over the handlebars, protecting my chest and torso from wind and rain. I began wishing for coarse chip road, it's slow, but at least the water drains. I was done with the rain. By this stage I would have traded it for anything; hills, a headwind, more hills? The lush surrounding hills were a stark contrast to the dry plains a few days ago. This was not a dry part of Turkey. It was green, and it was wet.

One handed jobs were impossible, with the poncho, but at least my torso nearly stayed dry. Water from below couldn't be avoided, even with my bag acting as a rear mud guard. I was warm enough, as long as I kept moving. And given that I was trying to race around the world by bicycle, I was always moving.

The long 276 km day to Trabzon included several more deadly tunnels. I was so sick of the rain by this point that the tunnels became almost havens, of peace. Stopping briefly in the large city of Sansun I added more Turkish newspaper and plastic bags to the personal litter collection that was keeping me insulated.

Warm Showers hosting was rare in Turkey but Jennie at mission control had arranged for me to stay with a guy named Mustafa in Trabzon. It had been a bastard of a day, and after such a drowning, I really felt like just crashing at a hotel whatever the cost. The hotels had been affordable. I needed time alone, time to dry out, maintain my gear and body, and get some sleep. That would be the last thing that would happen.

Mustafa had kindly responded to my texts. It would have been rude to let him down at this stage. Moments before finding his apartment, I received a message saying he had a meeting at university. A friend of his would meet me and sure enough a young student named Nadim called out my name. He ushered me into a crowded student flat near the Trabzon University. The scene resembled an Otago scarfie gathering. A couple of flats had come together, girls and boys all flirting or watching football. Nobody was drinking Speights or any alcohol for that matter, but everyone was heavily smoking.

Soaking wet, I wasn't in the mood for cultural exchanges but Nadim was already introducing me to the numerous Turkish scarfies. I was trapped. Where the hell was the fabled Mustafa? He told me an hour? I thought about excusing myself for a hotel but by this stage Nadim had kindly loaned me some warm clothes. I didn't want to appear rude.

The students were friendly and curious about the very wet westerner on a strange machine. They offered me food for which I was grateful but communication was difficult, I just wanted sleep, and I needed to prepare for tomorrow. I recognised the bizarre situation would one day make a great story and tried to accept the experience.

There would no time left tonight for maintenance and was a painful three hours before the charismatic looking Mustafa finally showed up. Conversation was finally possible but Mustafa was in no hurry to go home, he sat down and joined the smoking. An hour later we finally headed to Mustafa's flat where it seemed the smoking party would continue. Mustafa apologised that the heating was off. I felt like crying.

After about three hours sleep, I put on wet cycling clothes, filled them with fresh dry rubbish, and headed off 200 km toward Hopa where Mustafa had warned me about gangsters. It continued to rain. The puncture gods joined in the bullying with two in quick succession, no surprise given the amount of dirt on the roads. Needless to say I was getting pissed off. I set about addressing the problems methodically but there was no doubt the tantrums were intensifying. This rain was hating me, drowning me and ruining my stuff. On the upside; I was close to beating Turkey.

I woke in Hopa, 20 km from the Georgian town of Batumi. It was still raining. Turkey had not been kind to me and I was eager to get out. Customs was fairly straightforward; I was only sent to four different places before entering my 18th country of the trip. I had finally beaten Turkey and I gave the sky the finger.

It was as if the weather recognised borders and the sun came out as I crossed the border into the Black Sea Georgian city of Batumi. Both my rear lights had been drowned and I had been running out of repair patches. I found a bike shop of sorts in the potholed streets. The faces had instantly reverted to a more Eastern European look.

One of the first sights that I encountered sent my mind back to New Zealand...rugby posts! Coincidently, the All Blacks were playing Georgia in the 2015 Rugby World Cup that very day. The final score was 43 - 10. To the All Blacks, of course, but go Georgia! Not bad considering the small population, limited infrastructure and no spare funding for sport. At first glance it was obvious that people were too busy here trying to survive to care about rugby.

The buildings also reverted to the Eastern European style; dull, concrete and unkept. It was obvious I had entered a new land. The ancient

Georgian script was fascinating and completely illegible. Just before I headed inland I met a Japanese cycle tourist, Kenji, who had been riding through Armenia and Azerbaijan and camping the whole time. Manly points.

It was absolute bliss to ride in sunshine, I'd forgotten what it felt like. I turned inland onto a beautiful single lane country road with limited traffic alongside a river, the scenery not dissimilar to the Motueka Valley. Cows roamed along the road while Babushkas gathered wood for the approaching winter. What a contrast to the misery of the last few days. Surely I couldn't be enjoying myself? As it grew dark, I skirted the town of Samtredia looking for the hostel that had accepted my online booking the previous night.

Frequent creaks were coming from the bottom bracket. This is a sure sign of mechanical illness. I hoped the issue would go away but bikes have poor immune systems and don't get better by themselves. There would be few, if any, bike doctors in Georgia who could treat this ailment. This was a bad time and a bad place for a problem of that scale. Bottom bracket issues are serious. Creaks are usually caused by exposure to water and dirt and there had been plenty of both in recent days. Creaks usually lead to a complete collapse, but at times it can mean there's just a little water, and then the noise subsides. I hoped it would go away, and I pretended not to hear.

It turned out the hostel that took my booking the night before was only a summer thing. I had to backtrack a few kilometres to Samtredia where I hoped I could find a hotel. I found a shop that sold six things. I bought one of each, some manky bread, a Russian looking Nutella type substitute, a packet of dodgy biscuits and a tin of something like baby food which I later threw out. I added a bottle of water and a bottle of vodka which were about the same price. I'd often calm the nerves in Europe with a beer or two but in Turkey alcohol was rare or expensive. The rain and mountains had certainly frayed my nerves; I deserved a good stiff drink.

I drew plenty of stares in the downtown area and felt uncomfortable. Samtredia had been one of the major battlegrounds in the Georgian Civil War and it looked tired, beaten up and angry. I eventually found a hotel of sorts and a helpful receptionist with a hump showed me to an upstairs room.

"Never, never, never give up."
Winston Churchill

The previous afternoon's brief respite was to be the calm before the storm. Within 20 minutes of leaving Samtredia my bottom bracket had collapsed. The wind picked up and I was bouncing along on a pot holed and dangerous road. I had virtually no food, then my seat post bolt broke. I had needed to ride up a massive mountain, and fix two punctures. Tantrums were put aside, I had a serious potential race ender to deal with. I focused on efficiently dealing with the smaller tasks and kept moving, I wouldn't give up. In 1995, my Olympic long track dream had begun to falter, and I hadn't give up then.

Jim Morrison's 'The End' was hardly the most positive track to place in my head, as realistic as it was. I replaced it with another Led Zeppelin classic: "Crying won't help you, praying won't do you no good, when the levee breaks, mama, you got to move".

After my successful first long track season, the going got tough. The beginnings of true professionalism were becoming obvious amongst the larger skating nations. The natural result was an increase in the overall world standard. The next three seasons would be a challenge. My technical faults had been firmly ingrained from years of short track, but I knew what I was looking for and there was plenty of video analysis. I consciously focused on technical cues, but old habits were proving difficult to iron out. It was becoming hard to teach an old dog new tricks.

I was unable to reach the high level of

expectations I had for set for myself after the first season. There were more losses than wins as I continued backpacking from one world cup to another. Failures were frequent, and wins, just the tip of the iceberg. While everyone else improved, I was stagnating or getting squashed. I did my best hopping between Calgary and Norway where I picked up the language. My Norwegian girlfriend supported my goals, making training in Norway possible. A couple of times I returned to New Zealand to scrounge up a few dollars in the off season. But by the 1997-1998 Olympic qualifying season I hadn't had a summer for 12 years, the lack of daylight perhaps adding to the overall depression. I wouldn't quit! I had made a promise.

Making it backpacker style required huge compromises. With short track, training in New Zealand was less than ideal, but it was possible. Skating at the top end in long track came with the expenses of living abroad. It was a constant financial strain. The stress continued to hinder my performance, especially over the longer distances.

I was never able to be in one place long enough to seriously make money and my mediocre results were reflected in my ever declining Sports Foundation grants. The top 20 in World Cup Competition made reasonable prize money but after 20th it dropped away to nothing. I was just out of range and my meagre savings from the occasional coaching work soon dried up. Getting to events became a sea of compromise. As the sport became more and more professional, I compromised more, simply to stay on the circuit. It became like a highly stressful job only without pay. Three years later it was marginal as to whether I would even qualify for Nagano but I continued to give it my best with what I had. Quitting wasn't an option.

A few months out from the 1998 winter Olympics, I stepped up to the line in a World Cup 1000m race for one final chance to meet the strict Olympic qualifying time. My technique had barely improved but I'd get there on anger and brute force, I'd turn the race into one almighty tantrum.

It may not have looked pretty but I got there in 1:13.63; well under the Olympic qualifying time of 1:16. Elated, I felt a huge sense of relief and pride. I would be the first New Zealander to compete in a Long Track Olympic Competition, and the first in history to compete in short track and then long track. It had been an immense physical, financial and emotional struggle, but I had stuck it out and I would make it to a third Olympics in a sport where no New Zealander should ever have stepped foot.

The New Zealand Olympic committee couldn't have a skater turn up to an Olympic Games without a coach, they would have to fork out for someone. But New Zealand didn't have a long track coach. I'd been the first to seriously do the sport and had so far managed on my own.

The New Zealand Olympic Committee sensibly gave me free pickings and a Canadian skater/coach named Lester Pardoe was the obvious choice. During my last two seasons I had trained frequently with Lester, who had only narrowly missed out on Olympic qualification himself. Just outside the Canadian squad, Lester trained independently and became my ideal training partner. A mature athlete with a sense of humour reminiscent of my old short track team, Lester took some of the stress away from training.

Just out of reach of Canadian funding, Lester had also made huge financial sacrifices to keep his Olympic dream alive. We were both dead broke when officially announced as part of the New Zealand Olympic team. Making the team didn't mean any extra money. All Lester and I would get was an air ticket and fancy clothing once we got there.

I shared a basement suite at his parent's house in the months before Nagano. Lester kept training in hope that a Canadian might be injured. We lived like students on next to nothing. Every cent had to be managed, we bought food in bulk and would live on large portions of cheap, nutritious chilli, veggies and rice. On one occasion we destroyed a massive bulk cook up. Instead of the usual seasoning sachets we added an equal portion of cheaper pure chilli powder. It was deadly, barely edible but throwing it out was not an affordable option. Cycling to the track through the snow we would whistle Johnny Cash's 'Ring of Fire' - it became our theme song.

The University of Calgary eating halls also provided relatively cheap food for students and starving athletes. Serve yourself plates of pasta were only $2.99 but the plates were small. We pushed the boundaries, with pasta and sauce overflowing onto the tray, the cashier threatened to charge us double. We created strategies to maximise volume. By layering and cementing the mixture with free parmesan cheese, we learned to build upwards. The pile soon resembled a top hat. As long as it stayed on the plate it was still only $2.99. Having to compromise on food was hardly ideal preparation for an Olympic athlete.

In a pre-Olympic event in Germany we turned a financial hurdle into a profit by making and selling a 'silly lap board'. In long track speed skating the coach's role is to hold up a swanky digital 'lap board' to encourage skaters to keep lap times steady. With large crowds, yelling out the lap time doesn't work, you need a board. 9 7 for example would indicate a 29.7 second lap.

Neither the Olympic Committee or New Zealand Federation had a lap board, Lester and I would have to make one. We went to the local stationary shop, buying up 20 large sheets of cardboard and a black pen. We started doodling silly pictures and stylising the numbers. The 0 was a smiley face, number 2 was represented by a rattlesnake. The 3 was a horizontal set of sizeable boobs. We were onto something and went back to the store and spent a little extra. We added tinsel, balloons and glitter. It was christened 'the silly lap board', for it was silly.

Lester with the 'Silly Lap Board'

My 5000m race was on live TV. Any lap

eliciting the numeral 3 would draw an extra-large cheer from the Dutch crowd. The Germans didn't get it. The silly lap board was sold to a collector for 100 euros, meaning we could eat until we got to the sanctuary of Olympic Village.

I became a true celebrity during the Nagano games. I was far from medal potential by this stage but I made a great story of interest. Speed skating was a major sport for the Japanese. The self-coached and majorly underfunded skater from New Zealand became a curiosity for the media. With my smattering of Japanese I conducted several interviews. The focus on how I got there led to greatly appreciated donations. It was bizarre. Perhaps it was my poor Japanese but the media made out that I carved my own skates out of bone, lived in a cave and got to Nagano by a canoe.

Walking around the city I became recognised and mobbed by fans. Lester and I took the opportunity to sell off much of our Olympic clothing and the Olympic pins we were given. We walked away in T-shirts, with what we considered a small fortune!! The Chef de Mission was horrified. It was embarrassing at the final team photo session, when I had to be shunted to the back. The team cashmilon trench coat had been sold to a Japanese fan for the equivalent of a few night's accommodation. But I planned to skate out the remainder of the season after the Olympics and I needed the money.

The snow sports athletes on my team would likely savour their mementos in drawers. Perhaps never to be seen or worn again? Mine were quickly flogged off to keep the dream alive. Many of my Nagano team mates were not of the calibre of my old speed skating team.

The New Zealand media often portrays the Winter Olympics as a snow holiday for skiers with rich parents, and in many cases this is true. Not so in the case of the Albertville and Lillehammer relay team, and certainly not the case for my Nagano Games. We were as strong, fit and driven as any Kiwi athlete in any sports code. What's more, we did it without funding, support or recognition.

I had sacrificed everything, in every aspect of life, to get to Nagano. My last Olympic Games was built on blood, sweat and tears. I gave it my all and then some to get to there.

A top 20 was not unrealistic but I ended 35th in the 1000m. I finished toward the tail end of the field but I was a genuine competitor. In a brutal sport I had had to meet strict qualifying times and overcome enormous emotional, physical and financial hurdles. I had more than earned my right to compete at my third Olympics.

New Zealand's first Long Track Speed Skating Olympian Andrew Nicholson, Nagano 1998, 1500m

I gave up skating once and for all midway through the 2000 season. I had considered an attempt at qualifying for Salt Lake Games but it wasn't working out. I'd run out of money to do it backpacker style.

Although the complete lack of funding and support may have limited my potential as an athlete there were other benefits. The self-coached, scrape, scrounge and compromise style certainly taught me to stretch a dollar. It taught me to become resourceful, hardworking and to think for myself. It also added a sense of complete ownership of the achievement. I experienced travel adventures, not just sports trips. My Nagano preparation gave me the skills to take on my world ride

By contrast, athletes who grow up in environments that cater for their every whim are less likely to gain such skills or insights. They become products of an athlete factory, tools of the trade for their nation's sports programmes. In cultures where everyone is special, they also often become spoilt brats.

By trying to get to the Nagano Olympics, I had been trying to pull off the impossible. Things had got tough back then, but I never quit. I wouldn't quit on day 67 of my world ride either. I would control the controllable. I got through the day and finally, I managed to get out a plea for help.

Facebook message sent to Jennie Sat 17 Oct

> *'Hi Jen, major issue, bottom bracket ruined, bike still ridable will try to limp to Tbilisi tomorrow ETA 3pm. Will need replacement fitted before Indian flight Monday morning? Let me know if you can find anyone who can help. The thing I am most proud about was how uncharacteristically calm I have been ? I am wondering if that was the personal learning point of this trip? I don't know if it is realistic to afford and be able to sort the above, I will try. There's people out there with bigger problems, i'll see what can be done... shame'*

The cell coverage overnight had disappeared and I had no idea whether a possible solution had been found as I rolled out of the dull city of Gori. I swallowed two caffeine tablets as breakfast one and began *'kathunking'* the remaining 90 km towards the capital Tbilisi. I correctly guessed that the strong cold Easterly blast would continue and progress was painfully slow, as expected. An hour or two after sunrise I found a shop. This one only sold four things but one resembled potato chips which served as breakfast two. I passed several depressingly backward villages which would have looked little different 100 years ago. Outside the city, horses and carts were still the only affordable transport for many villagers. Several spooky looking castles remained on strategically defensive hilltops, and ruins both new and old dotted the countryside. Oppressed, this place had been bullied by bigger neighbours for years.

It was only mid-Autumn but it was already cold. It was hard to comprehend that things would not get warmer for months to come. The Indian poor I was expecting to encounter may have it tough, but at least they wouldn't freeze. The surrounding brown countryside here would soon be covered with white.

As I approached the busy streets of Tbilisi I passed a western looking hotel that I guessed correctly would likely have Wi-Fi. There was a promising message from Jennie. *'Head for Tbilisi Extreme, ask for Lado.'* I bookmarked the shop and followed the star.

Just as I rolled up to the shop I encountered a scruffy looking Western cycle tourist who I correctly guessed was English. His name was Alex and I would get to know him well over the next few hours. Alex was staying at the backpackers / bike shop of 'King Lado'. Lado had been expecting me!

Lado was Georgia's Mr Cycling. A motivated, entrepreneurial man, who had been a professional soccer player. He was way more comfortable financially than the average Georgian and ran the bike shop and a backpackers as a side-line business. He had got Jennie's message and had already called in his mechanic for some overtime. He shook my hand and set his mechanic to work on my bike. He had one bottom bracket on the shelf that would fit my bike, the only one in Georgia.

Saved by Tbilisi Extreme

Lado even charged me a reasonable fee. I couldn't believe my luck, not only was my bike being fixed but I also had a bed for the night. I scrounged a bike box and some tape for the morning, and after a few hours' sleep, made my way 20 km to the Tbilisi airport with a bike box tucked under my arm. The major mechanical breakdown that I believed would end the record had been sorted in a jiffy.

By a miracle I was suddenly on the transfer flight to India, and somehow still in the game. I was behind on the record, with the toughest leg of journey about to begin and the clock constantly running, yet I remained in the amazing race and still had a chance to both survive, and to break the record. I took a deep breath and after a huge McDonald's feast in my transfer at Dubai, I managed two hours plane sleep before touching down in India. The race continued.

Chapter 11

India

In India, I would have support for four days. The riding would be tough but I would have help where and when I needed it most. The Turkish drownings and Georgian bike crisis had been overcome but I was still behind the record. I was also about to enter the toughest leg of the trip and I was certainly grateful for any assistance.

It had been organised that a young 23 year old roller skating coach named Akshay would accompany me by motorcycle, for around four days, heading east from Mumbai. I had never met

Akshay. Everything had been sorted through an Indian friend I had in Auckland named Amol. Amol was involved with the Hauraki Ice Racing Club, he had arranged everything.

Before Amol had emigrated to New Zealand, he and his young son Aryan had been involved in roller skating in Mumbai. Coincidently, Akshay and I had both coached young Aryan, an Indian/Kiwi ice and roller speed skater who was now growing up in West Auckland. A fascinating example of how time, Facebook and just a few degrees of separation can create unusual connections and encounters.

It was 3:00am, but the thick heat wave and smell of India shook me into a state of alertness as I exited the arrival hall. I recognised Akshay from his Facebook photo. I shook his hand and with a shy smile Akshay introduced me to a friend who had borrowed his parent's car to shuttle me the few kilometres to Akshay's home, the official start of Leg 3 near Marve Beach. I collapsed on a mat laid out for me in the main family room, surrounded by the rest of his sleeping family.

After a short but deep four hours sleep I awoke to a new world. I was introduced to Akshay's sister and parents, middle class Mumbaikars who welcomed me into their tidy and modest home. Akshay's dad was nearing retirement from a lengthy career in the Indian Navy. His mum cooked me us up some 'upma', a mildly spicy Indian breakfast staple and what would be a most excellent cycling fuel.

Akshay hurried his mother along while I assembled my bike and chatted with his sister. She wore a fashionable cycling jersey. The next 10 million Indian women I would see would mostly be dressed in traditional saris. Akshay knew we couldn't hang around, he strapped my bag to his motor bike and we were off! Amol, it seemed, had arranged the right guy to help me out of Mumbai.

Akshay Kumble and Andrew Nicholson ready to take on India

Having a guide was a godsend. Akshay and his family were doing better than the average Indian but Akshay had still never travelled beyond his home state of Maharashtra. This was a major adventure for Akshay, but he confidently began leading me out of this massive city. A speed skating coach and part time student, Akshay was shy, but as an athlete and a coach in a tough sport, he understood the urgency of our mission.

Leg Three of the amazing race had begun in a flash, it was focus time! We hit the road and the heat, noise and traffic was immediate and intense. I'd ridden in the madness of India before, taking a trip down the western coast in 2001. For the moment, however, I paid little attention to detail. I was back in the race and making the most of the support.

The plan was simple. Follow the yellow helmet and get out of Mumbai! Akshay would ride 10 - 20 metres ahead. Direct drafting was against the rules and would have been extremely dangerous but we kept each other in close sight. The road was alive, the horns were blasting and as predicted, India was bombarding all the senses. Total concentration was required.

The roads out of Mumbai could have been classified as motorways but their contents are slower and more varied compared to the west. On my far right honked rusted overloaded trucks, highly unsafe looking buses and a few cars. Ranks of standard yellow and black three-wheel auto rickshaws also buzzed past, somewhat closer. In my immediate riding zone was the weaker of the road, things that didn't matter, like small motorbikes, other bicycles, donkey drawn transport and western cycle racers. To my left were millions of busy pedestrians, along with dogs and cows rummaging through the endless piles of plastic and rotting garbage.

Horn use is encouraged in India. They love it and use it, and this makes good sense. As with most of Asia, horn blasting is not meant as abuse. It is a simple and appropriate warning to 'get out of the way or die'. The warning is appreciated, usually headed and the system works. Horn blasting varies greatly in volume and enthusiasm.

The traffic thickened as I entered the visible pollution haze of the main highway. The sound of horns became one long drone as I chased Akshay east towards the Ghats. The road surface was smooth but large chunks were often missing, and cracks between concrete slabs could be dangerous.

After a few sprints over busy overbridges, I failed to spot a large crack in the road. The beloved five Euro thruster pump, that I had carried since Germany, bounced from my frame and into the middle of the lane. I pulled over, waiting with the faint hope that a gap in the traffic would appear and the pump could be retrieved in one piece. Pointing frantically at the pump, I waved at approaching traffic. I needed that pump in India, presta valves would be hard to find.

The first two trucks straddled the pump, a following rickshaw swerved, missing it by inches. The drivers action was more out of surprise at the frantically gesturing white man, than any deliberate intention to avoid hitting my precious possession. But Pumpy's days were numbered and the following truck squashed it to pieces, much to the amusement of the truck's human cargo.

The pump was ruined and Akshay got a chance to witness the first of what would be many Indian tantrums. I took some deep breaths and the opportunity to take a memory snap of the scene, we were directly outside Mumbai's Cricket Stadium.

It took a good four hours before we were truly out of Mumbai, and this part of India was by no means flat. We were soon climbing over a huge Ghat; through a tunnel and heading east. The tunnel reminded me of Turkey, only the sewage drain was completely open, the tunnel was darker and the road in far worse condition. I rode carefully but with confidence.

By now my face was already black from the morning's pollution. I emerged from the tunnel of death looking like I'd been working in a coal mine and smelling like I'd worked in a sewer. We veered south towards Pune. Now rolling gently downhill and with traffic thinning, I let out yelp of excitement! I was in a bike race like none other! It was mad, I was truly living. I had beaten Mumbai! The race may have been the most intense challenge of my life, but for brief moments I felt a rush of excitement as I recognised the scale what I was doing. At times I was actually loving it.

In spite of the lack of sleep, the unavoidable late start and intense heat and traffic, Akshay and I had made nearly 200 km as we pulled up to a hotel approaching to Pune. I high fived him as we entered the lobby, encouraging him to feel part of the achievement, as he was.

I'd barely had a chance to meet Akshay, who I had trusted completely. We had hit India running and had beaten Day 1, or 71. It would have been a nightmare to tackle Mumbai alone. I would have been lucky to get out alive. I started to get to know Akshay over an aloo gobi at the hotel and prepared my gear for a second day of mayhem.

I was going to be in India longer than I had originally planned. My original route had me entering Iran from Turkey, but due to visa complications I opted for a shorter leg, allowing a hop to Mumbai by plane from Georgia. I couldn't find any negative reports from cycle tourists who had visited Iran and I was disappointed to be missing it. But my flight from the much smaller former Soviet state of Georgia meant that I had kilometres to make up for elsewhere, and some of that distance would have to done in India.

Due to the various crises, I had also been forced to take more direct routes than planned, in order to catch my Tbilisi flight. I was running out of planet in which to travel east. I could go southeast or even south, but I couldn't go west, Guinness rules forbade it. To make up for lost kilometres I would now have to dogleg south in India, where less than ideal riding conditions were inevitable. I had 16 days left to get in as many kilometres as possible, going any direction other than west, and get to Kolkata.

Shortly after an early start on Day 2 of India, Akshay detoured off the main highway to central Pune to try and find a new pump. The pump issue didn't warrant the tantrum I threw as I had bought with me a Presta-Schrader valve adapter. At frequent intervals along main Indian roads numerous 'air-wallahs' sat patiently by an air hose. For 10 rupees, the air-wallah would crank up a smoky generator by which passing vehicles could top up their tyres. Even easier than my euro thruster. At about NZ 10 cents, even I wasn't too cheap to make daily use of this fantastic service.

It was essential to make the most of Akshay's support while it lasted. He would proudly lead the way, at times riding ahead to negotiate both food and accommodation. For the next three days, I simply focused on his western style Barcelona football jacket and bright yellow helmet. As we headed into more rural India, even Akshay stood out from the millions dressed in white along on the busy roadside. I must have looked like a complete alien. Spectators who gathered on motorbikes were directed to Akshay, who explained our mission in either Hindi or Maharashtrian. For a couple of brief hours each evening I enjoyed getting to know Akshay over a curry and talk about skating.

For four days, I peddled, he guided. We stopped to eat occasionally at various establishments, where even the cricket series between India and South Africa was dropped in favour of viewing the western bike tourist. It takes something quite unusual to draw Indians away from a close cricket match.

Anytime that we dismounted in a noisy, overcrowded main street of a city or town, we were immediately swamped by a sea of curious spectators. The people behind them were just waiting to pounce and do that which Indians do best: form a crowd. If I were to stop for just a moment at a fruit stall, an instant crowd would gather. For the moment, I had my manager Akshay to take some of the focus off me. He would proudly explain the Guinness world record attempt while I would cower in the corner, trying my best to get in some much needed calories, whatever the risk. Upon turning to leave, I would be surprised at how popular the eatery had just become. We would have to battle our way through the crowd to open space, to get back to our bikes.

Akshay had guided me nearly 1,000 km south east toward Zaheerabad. On my last night with Akshay, we indulged in a feast of fantastic curries and Kingfisher beer. Akshay relaxed significantly and shared a long list of tough ailments that had restricted his skating. He was a tough athlete but bad luck had restricted his own goals. He was having to settle for coaching, I felt sorry for him. It was a sad goodbye. Akshay was going to take his time to get home and visit some temples along the way.

I would have to manage the rest of India alone. Any tourist to India experiences the 'people factor,' but it is bicycle tourists who bear the full brunt. Cycling through remote, less travelled, mono-cultural areas make the cyclist a lone exotic species in a sea of sardines. Sitting for dinner in a timber shed eating chapatti or dal, I felt like I was in a human zoo. Curious eyes filled the street outside, peering at the strange creature from a faraway land. Never wavering, they followed every rip and dip of the soft, dal bread I gorged myself on. The dhaba-wallah (restaurant owner) had to keep pushing people out the door as they crept closer and closer to investigate.

Akshay had been carrying my bag for the last four days, and I immediately felt the added weight as the headwind strengthened and I headed east. I had planned to bypass India's fourth biggest city, Hyderabad, via what looked like a newly built ring road. Having ridden through Mumbai and on other highways, I assumed that bicycles and all traffic were pretty much permitted to run the risk of riding wherever they dared in India. I assumed nobody bothered with safety rules of any sort here, ever. I approached the toll gate but, "no bike, no bike" the toll officer yelled, as I entered the newly built ring road. This road appeared to be an exception to the anything anywhere rule, and I was directed back to the main central road.

The only option was to ride directly through the middle of this colossal city with a massive 'nufus' of eight million. Worse still, I had to take the long skinny way. Finding small roads through the city would have only led to a labyrinth of chaos.

Risking other roads around Hyderabad would have probably led to disastrous road surfaces. Away from the main highways, Indian roads are a wreck. I had encountered potholed chaos in some long and unavoidable sections of the last few days. The main road up the guts, around 50 km, was the best way to get through Hyderabad. I braced for the worst.

The battle of Hyderabad had begun. It was going to be hot, crazy and long! With the temperature already well into the late-thirties, heat mixed with the pollution which had been visible for miles. The build-up of the diverse and highly unsafe traffic began to intensify. I resigned myself to a few hours of madness. The road ahead would probably be the single most challenging task of the entire trip. Like Mumbai, the blasts of horns mingled into one long load drone. The constant stench of garbage mixed with the increasing smell of engine pollution, only occasionally interrupted by the smell of exotic incense. Pedestrian explosions from leap frogging buses began. The bus drivers and pedestrians were even more erratic and unpredictable than those in Turkey. The litter and pollution increased as I passed large areas of dense slums and a sea of tarpaulins and corrugated iron.

Given time, when cycling in India the unpredictability becomes predictable. Traffic can and will do anything. That's why you keep sharp. I switched on the total concentration button.

Recognising the extent of the challenge, it was during the battle of Hyderabad that I experienced what was probably the most amazing sense of flow in my life. With the extreme demands of the task I naturally became more focused. I abandoned the idea of a tantrum and sensibly accepted the situation. I assumed my place in the food chain of the road and began riding confidently through Hyderabad.

The key to survival was to assertively behave like a local on a small motorbike. My size and speed were roughly equivalent, so I could bully lesser cyclists, pedestrians and dogs. Likewise, anything bigger could bully me at their leisure. Might is right. This was the caste system on wheels. The logical law of the jungle. I had seen enough of Indian roads to know that auto rickshaws are perfectly entitled to cut me off. I should accept this as normal and without complaint.

The only exception to the might is right rule in India is the holy cow. Cows are the joker of the pack. They trump everything! Even trucks and buses must and do yield to India's numerous holy cows. It's truly mental!

Traffic eddies form on the major highways in India. When the traffic in the main flow gets heavy, other traffic may choose to travel towards you in their opposite shoulder. It seems it's perfectly acceptable to ride in the shoulder going the opposite direction, if you were just going down the road.

I rode boldly, held my line where appropriate and applied the 'give way to anything bigger' rule. In my Hyderabad flow state, I cycled with my head down, eyes ahead and fingers ready at the brakes. I entered a state of consciousness whereby all that existed was me, my bike and the road. All else; people, animals, vehicles, were of no significance, merely obstacles to be avoided. Cycling through Hyderabad I drew on the skills of a short track speed skater. Ready for anything, from any direction. I was riding confidently and assertively, in the zone, and I came through the battle of Hyderabad unscathed and victorious.

Everyone assumes that cycling in places like India is suicide, but this is nonsense. The varied and erratic traffic might increase the chances of a slow speed tumble, but the chances of getting killed outright while riding in New Zealand is probably higher! The obvious difference is speed. I'd sooner ride across Hyderabad then cross a narrow bridge on an open New Zealand road. A milk container bearing down on you from behind, a logging truck from the front. There is little margin for error and with 200 kph of speed to consider, if things go wrong, you're dead!

As I entered the countryside again, I got a puncture, but hid in a drain before anyone spotted me; favouring sewage, shade and quiet over heat and mobbings. I was coping in India alone, I had a good warm up, prior experience, bike and mental skills. I was holding onto the record even in the worst of conditions. I was looking after the process and the result was looking after itself.

It was clear that this section of the Hyderabad Vijayawada Highway had only recently been completed. The relatively good surface and wide shoulder nearly compensated for the ever-present headwind. Several toll stations are spread along this highway and bicycles at least, are permitted to bypass the toll gates on the left. Everyone else must pay...with a few exceptions; the elite, the Union Minister, government officials etc. Basically, the few who could afford to pay, didn't have to; and the millions who couldn't afford to, did.

The World's biggest democracy

I rolled up to Chandapudni, calling it a day and desperately needing a place to sleep. I was attracting large crowds and had several frustrating and confusing conversations as I went back and forth along the main street trying to find anything that resembled a hotel.

The lines that define a 'hotel' in India, are not clear. A hotel can mean simply four plastic chairs around a table where dubious food is sometimes served. On one occasion a deceased human body lay wrapped near the tables, awaiting burial or cremation. The chef beckoned me over to sit and eat, needless to say I declined. It reminded me the Faulty Towers episode where Basil and Manuel desperately tried to hide the body of a dead guest from other visitors. No such attempt had been made here. New Zealand Health and Safety may have had a problem with this arrangement.

I had become familiar with and even adopted the famous Indian 'head wobble', which was reward enough in itself. English may be the business language of India but even the words yes and no are not necessarily universally understood. The head wobble is a slight cock of the head to one side. It can mean 'yes' or 'no', 'hello' or 'goodbye', 'more please' or 'that's enough, thank you'. It takes a while to decipher the gesture correctly. This is made even more confusing because the accompanying vocalisation is neither a clear 'yes' or a clear 'no'... a kind of 'mnehr', "Is this a hotel"...(head wobble) "mnehr"... "So, no? yes? Can I sleep here?" After dozens of frustrating conversations I eventually found a room empty of corpses but complete with rat droppings for the bargain price of $4.

After a refreshing wash, I went out for a food hunt. Crowds, including a reporter, were already waiting for me. I had no idea how he had knowledge of my ride let alone my whereabouts. The uninhibited inquisitiveness shown by the locals was generally innocent, often endearing, and not at all surprising considering I may well have been literally the only westerner the locals had ever seen outside a TV screen. Regardless, for those whose personal space barely extends beyond the width of their own shoulders, knowing how to deal with it can be very difficult.

After a risky but tasty egg curry, I returned to my rat nest for maintenance duty. Up until now, Akshay had helped me source food, accommodation and some internet. He also reminded me of my duties toward Guinness and about keeping accurate records, but by this stage my mind was on surviving rather than the record. The list of jobs that needed doing was, as usual, extensive. What little time remained I used fixing daily punctures, pumping tyres, rinsing and wrestling with washing, and body and bike maintenance.

"Victory awaits him who has everything in order — luck, people call it. Defeat is certain for him who has neglected to take the necessary precautions in time; this is called bad luck."
Roald Amundsen

I had started to wonder if my adventure would make a good book, and on Facebook I had asked for suggestions on a title. Lester suggested, *'Stevie the Saddle Sore and Harry the Haemorrhoid's Grand World Tour.'* Amusing, but I had managed to avoid any significant saddle sores to this point. I attributed this to good management rather than good luck. Saddle sores are likely to occur with lengthy periods of time on the bike in humid conditions, and in the presence of bacteria filled environments. My 'saddle area' was therefore permanently in danger of becoming an open invitation for a saddle-sore fiesta. A decent sized saddle sore could do more than simply be uncomfortable, it could have ended the race. These pus-filled swellings have forced Tour de France riders to abandon. Failing to look after the saddle area was a recipe for disaster. It needed to be done, no matter what.

Daily I would thoroughly clean, and I carried and used saddle cream. Changing shorts regularly also increased the chances of avoiding these evil pus-filled infections, and that is exactly what I did. I had also experimented with a variety of bicycle seats before leaving, and favouring comfort over efficiency, I choose a women's touring seat ahead of the latest 50-gram carbon racer. I was going to be on the seat a while. I needed to be comfortable.

Carrying sufficient saddle cream and a second pair of shorts were more items that would weigh me down, but without them an infection would almost certainly emerge. Rarely had heaters worked in Eastern Europe or Turkish hotels, and the humidity in India or South East Asia made drying impossible. The time needed to clean shorts, followed by the necessity to wring out the chamois with the hotel towel, was a strength sapping and time consuming job. I could have simply not bothered. But I did bother, and I made my own luck. My ride would not end due to saddle sores, thanks to my diligent attention to potential problems.

I made my own luck in other ways. I carried a container of high dose Voltaren in anticipation of the inevitable hip, back or knee issues that would surely develop with the unprecedented amount of daily mileage required. But my joints were strong, stable and flexible as result of consistent strength and flexibility work. I was as prepared as possible. A back ailment, or neglected and poorly managed knee injury, would have been another race ender; but I never needed to touch the painkillers.

My connective tissues, posture and strength were solid due to years of athletic preparation and competitive powerlifting. It wasn't luck that my joints and bones were holding out. I hadn't had a crash yet either, good luck or excellent focus? Years of short track speed skating and working with experienced and professional sports psychologists had helped me focus. I was making my own luck through good preparation. Years of it. Despite the strain, I was getting through this monumental challenge. I had been right to believe in myself. One day at a time.

Food was a constant priority, preferably safe food. Slowing down, only to move on again, the flies and sewer would often keep me moving as I scouted the various stalls and potential food sources along the busy and populated highways. The first priority is determining the safety factor. I followed the basics; water obviously needed to come from sealed bottles, no salads, and I avoided meat.

Judging by the flies and dead things, food was clearly going to be gamble in India, and I naturally became hygiene paranoid. Anyone who has travelled through India — particularly those on a budget in non-tourist areas — knows how difficult it is to stay healthy. And I was already in a state of

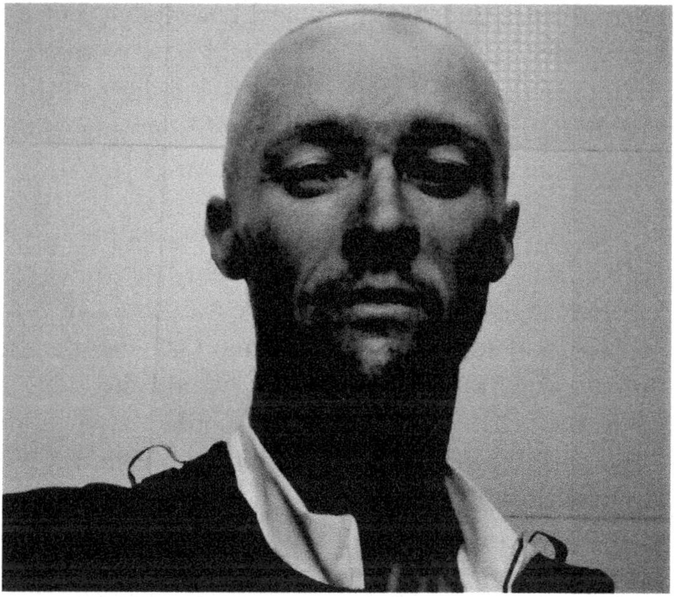

constant fatigue, sleep deprived, and needing to cover 240 km per day by bicycle.

My immune system was at its lowest, weakened, and the threat of illness loomed over my shoulder and made itself known with every twist, turn, and rumble of the stomach. And once invaded by a bug, it would be incredibly difficult to repel the occupying force and prevent further invasions. Eating three times as much as the average tourist probably tripled the chances of food poisoning, and in addition to the time spent eating, I needed to ride! Even a minor dose of Delhi Belly would have ended any chance of keeping the record in sight. Covering over 240 km on an empty stomach was not possible, however. I had to eat! I followed the normal rules and Akshay's local knowledge, but if I took every piece of advice I would have starved. I frequently bathed in hand sanitiser before putting my hands near food or mouth, another time consuming but necessary precaution.

Gear head cyclists would ask and assume I took power bars or some fanciful protein bar to get me through my trip, but firstly, there was no money for such products; and then, going fast meant the actual weight of the product would become a hindrance to performance. I could have gone through forty grunt bars a day! There was no way I could have carried that much fuel. This was an unsupported ride around the planet. Not the Taupo Half Ironman...I had to eat whatever I could find, frequently and on the run.

The road kill in India was taking both a tough heart and stomach. The occasional possum or flat hedgehog we see in New Zealand is nothing compared to riding past a dead donkey, bloated and maggot infested and decaying in the 35°C heat of the roadside shoulder. Long deceased dogs and various other animals make for a sad site. I wouldn't process sights like this. Just focus on the road, hold my breath and avoid the object. It was a problem I was too small to solve.

The next few days, routine developed, and the riding was brutal from start to finish. The road was always hot and I had had a constant head wind. The complete lack of time for organisation called for the necessity to do as many jobs as possible while actually still cycling. It was always better to be doing a job while rolling at 15 kph than not moving at all, but anything involving taking even one hand off the bars carries risk. Eating while riding was an obvious time saver, but depending on the type of food, this could be a frustrating and time consuming task. The only efficient way to both eat and ride was Cookie Monster style. Like Cookie Monster, a large portion of food gets dropped, but at five cents for a bag of chips even I could afford that loss. It would soon get scrounged by a stray dog and not go to waste.

It was important to pick traffic free moments to do moving bike jobs. Eating and struggling with awkward packaging is a dangerous task. Whenever possible, packaging would be opened and readied before riding. Although lacking in any nutrition, the small packets of potato chips were a safe, cheap and readily available food choice in India. The road side stalls that crossed the country could be counted on to sell soft drink, biscuits and small bags of potato chips which are low in nutrients but high in energy.

Chips, however, aren't easy to eat on the bike. I found that crushing the chips to near dust and simply pouring them in, was the most efficient way to get the petrol in the tank. Chip dust followed up with fizzy made up for a large portion of my calories. Even biscuits are best eaten crushed and poured. Easy to swallow options are always best, chewing takes time. There was no time to enjoy food, either on or off the bike. I needed to focus. Get the calories in and both hands back on the bars. This was a race, every second counted!

With care, sunblock and saddle cream could also be applied on the go, as could answering the call of nature. Admittedly it's not an easy task, but the skill improves with practice. Professional cyclists are experts and will agree that it is essential to determine the direction of the wind to avoid unpleasant backwash. I can't imagine how hard the call of nature must have been for Juliana Buhring, as a lone western women. How she coped in India alone is hard to imagine. One tough lady!

Navigation became a time consuming job and could be done on the bike if the phone was taped onto the aero bars. That is, assuming the sun was not blasting on the screen, making viewing impossible. Increasing the brightness setting would only waste essential battery power; everything was a compromise. Like driving while texting, any use of the phone in hand while riding massively increased the chance of either crashing or dropping the phone. The phone was my essential life line.

This $40 Huawei contained my navigation, accommodation details, contact with mission control, and emergency communication. Not to mention the Guinness-required images and videos. Breaking it would have spelt the end. I was always busy on the bike. As the logistical challenges increased, more had to be done on the move. There was little time for steady pedalling, I was always doing something. I would stretch at regular intervals whilst rolling on downhill sections, a task that was both necessary and required excellent bike handling skills.

The plan of taking a couple of hours of quiet in the peak of the afternoon sun was soon abandoned. Now, without Akshay, the mobbings were too hard to deal with. Without my manager, stopping in local eateries was simply not possible. The best way to get through India was as fast as possible, to start early and only take limited stops. If things went smoothly, a couple of hours shut in a 'hotel' may be possible at the end of a very long day. It was going to be a fight, I was already on the edge and I was still behind on the record. The reality was becoming that the bike, my body and my brain were all under increasing stress. The chances of a breakdown were high. India was pushing me to my limit! I would keep taking it one day at a time.

Although I was process oriented and working

through issues systematically, I was definitely starting to struggle emotionally and often failed to stay calm on the bike. Bursts of rage and frustration were increasing. I would have a tantrum and swear at the wind or traffic, only to later remind myself that it was just wasted energy. I wasn't keeping as calm as I had planned. I was stressing.

My cheap smartphone became a jumble of mostly blurred and rubbish pictures taken at bad angles while struggling on the bike. Flicking through them after the day from hell to Brahmapur, I noticed a 45 min video clip, showing the inside of my bike shirt. I had inadvertently began filming the inside my pocket. The visual was really boring, an empty packet of Indian chips being shuffled about, but the audio was hilarious. Over the constant blaring of horns, the dialog was still clearly audible.

> *"......FUCK!!....... Dumb fucken knob.........oh look at this moron ....GODDAMN PIG SLUT!!............THIS IS NOT A ROAD!!!!! ..... YOU CANNOT BE SERIOUS!!!!...... this FUCKIN road, he should be shot!.....SHOT!..."*

My angry voice calmed briefly, but inaudible muttering continues, something about the fuckin heat. The wind can then be heard increasing and the rant immediately surges up again, at full force.

> *"FUUUCK!!!!.....Fuck off!!.... Oh Fuckin wind eh?... 5 days Fuck!!..."*

I had recorded a good tantrum!

Early in the day, I occasionally opened up and greeted the countless locals on motorbikes who slowed to talk. I gathered as much enthusiasm as I could muster and answered all the usual, broken-English, interrogational questions:

"From which country?
"Your name?"
"Where do you go?"
"First time in India?"
"Brendan McCallum, cricket?"

As the heat increased and the day dragged on I would slowly lose patience with motor bike followers. I was in a foul mood and totally trashed. The wind had been cruel. It was scorching and as usual, all I'd eaten was potato chips and Fanta, just another day in India. On Day 77, having cycled in heat and wind for 11 hours and 230 km toward Rajahmundry, an angel came to help me.

All manner of unsafe vehicles were traveling alongside, to talk or simply stare. Motor bikes were the most common. As with most of Asia, there are no limits on how many persons per bike. Four was normal, especially for families, with children crammed into every available space. The motorbike flotilla I had attracted on this occasion was beginning to create a dangerous collective hazard for faster following traffic. I was the centre of that hazard and I didn't like it. The tantrum alert button flashed and the tension increased as the group of followers grew. I couldn't lose them. If I would slow down, the whole group of spectators would slow down. On this occasion, I had a full set of disciples. I felt like Brian from the Monty Python movie. To make the point that I wanted to be left alone, I would simply stop in hope that they would ride on. But if they hadn't finished looking, they would simply wait for me.

Even in India, many people own a smartphone. People wanted to stop and take selfies with me, constantly. Sometimes I obliged but usually I refused, I simply didn't have time. I tried not to be too much of an ugly tourist, but it was always toughest at the end of the day. The heat and fatigue had me wiped out by 3:00pm. As I approached the city this day, an extra-large flotilla was gathering and I was in no mood for it. The shortest answers possible would be given to the motorbike drivers, no elaboration, no eye contact. Basically I was starting to get rude. I would normally try to pre-mark hotels from Google Maps on my smartphone. I'd awkwardly navigate them in order to avoid any backtracking, hoping for a place to hide and sleep. More often than not they were only eating hotels, or even non-existent.

I knew I would eventually find something in Rajahmundry but it was likely to involve the usual miming games, head wobbling interpretation and frustrated conversations with the populous in the heat. I was only about 10 km out but I knew by now it would be some time before I was likely to get any peace. The motorbike riders continued to stare and pester me.

"What's your name?" came the usual first question from a follower on a Honda Hero... "John!" I snapped back, without even looking. 'Andrew' was hard for locals to pronounce. I figured a simpler name might help bypass the usual pronunciation lesson. I then curtly answered the remaining questions. 45, Kolkata, New Zealand! I was sick of hearing about Brendon McCullum's batting skills and paid no attention to the ramblings of the motorcyclist next to me.

"Do you need a hotel?" came a new question. This got my attention. I was suffering! Oh boy, did I need a hotel? I also needed peace, a cool shower and food; and fast. Clean would be probably be expecting too much but anything close would have done. But I certainly did not want to be taken to a place where people cooked food and stared at me from around a table. I cautiously asked the follower, "Can I sleep at this hotel? Is it a lodge?" "Yes, yes, it's good hotel near the main road, you follow me". I gave the follower my trust and warily agreed to let him guide me.

Deepu was his name, he was friendly and spoke good English. He explained how he worked with the local church and was some sort of peace monger. As a Christian, Deepu was certainly a minority in India. He told me how he had seen me when he was riding the other way. Apparently, God had told him to swing around and go and help me. I wasn't buying it, God had just given me a puncture and I'd had a head wind all day long. After all the names I'd been calling God the last few days, I didn't expect any help from him.

The conversation into the city was relaxed, and as promised, Deepu kindly lead me to a hotel just off the main road. It looked semi western, had the essential working Wi-Fi and the price was right. Deepu helped translate at reception and I was shown to a room that even looked clean. "Is it ok, John?" Deepu asked. Deepu had saved me time and stress and I had an immediate guilt attack, thinking back to my attitude when I had bluntly introduced myself as John only 30 minutes ago. Deepu refused any payment for his help. He received nothing from the hotel. There was nothing in it for him. He was just kind, even when I had started out rude. Deepu the Angel? Deepu had said he would meet me at 5:30am the next morning but he never showed up? Perhaps God had sent him on a more urgent mission?

I plodded north east, the headwind and heat continued. Unusually for India, there was a long gap between water stops. By midday I needed to rehydrate really soon. Eventually a shop of sorts appeared and I quickly gulped down two litres of water from a plastic receptacle at a roadside stall. I gestured to the owner as to what I should do with the offending piece of rubbish? He gestured to the ground. Throw it on the ground of course? The rubbish bin concept has yet to take off in India? I didn't have time to solve India's litter problem, I threw the plastic on the ground as directed and kept riding.

Since Vancouver I had made a personal rule of never intentionally littering. In Europe I would often end the day with manky plastic bags, chocolate bar wrappers and cans stuffed down my jersey and in my bike shorts or leggings. In the cooling temperatures the litter efficiently doubled as insulation. I was trying to make as little impact on the planet as possible. The environmentally friendliness of the bicycle was another passionate message I hoped I could one day share. In India, I abandoned this rule and littered like a trooper. Trying to solve the plastic problem in India was pointless, the problem was too big. Being a tidy Kiwi was lost cause. Interestingly however, broken glass is rare in India, as bottles can be recycled for money. Ahh?

I was proud to have so far survived any gut related illnesses. My iron stomach was getting me through the numerous digestive and intestinal stuff which more often than not incapacitates westerners. Unfortunately, however, I'd picked up both a nasty eye and a toe infection. Neither was surprising, given the unsanitary conditions those body parts were exposed to. I wouldn't escape India completely in one piece.

Before departure I had carefully considered the footwear question. My choice of footwear was a toss-up between a mountain bike shoe-pedal combo, or more efficient road shoes and a second pair of footwear. Unlike road shoes, mountain bike shoes are tough and designed to be both walked and cycled in. Walking in road shoes is like walking on ice, you are forced to waddle like a penguin but with less control. You can't help but bring attention to yourself by doing a terrible tap dance as you walk, and what's more, it ruins the cleat. Nonetheless I opted for road shoes and bungeed a light pair of jandals to my bag. The days were to be spent on the bike, not walking around. I needed maximum efficiency on the bike and road racing shoes provided this. If I had to walk more than a few steps, I'd use my jandals.

But in hindsight, walking around the gutters of trash and open sewers with unprotected toes was stupid. The slightest skin opening would be exposed to all manner of nasties. It was towards the end of India that my small right toe swelled and pulsed. It was extremely uncomfortable in my sweaty bike shoe which was probably the worst place for a pus filled infected toe to spend 13 hours. Sensibly I made the effort to tend to it. I used every available antiseptic, cleaned it and changed the dressing regularly. I even cut a small hole in the shoe to make room for the swelling. All this was time consuming and extreme care had to be taken to keep it covered and protected when venturing out. I monitored it closely and it eventually subsided. Again, perhaps I made my own luck.

I was in no mood to muck about with cleaning, soaking, rinsing and cutting dressings but this was a critical moment in the race. I recognised it and controlled it. Like rinsing and changing bike shorts. My muscles were showing they could do this thing but the rest of the system needed to be managed. This may have been the difference from me of 20 years ago when I would have been more inclined to ignore such issues.

I also didn't muck about when I saw my right eye in the mirror. My face always looked a state at the end of a day. Black with pollution, drawn and haggard. My eyes were usually somewhat bloodshot, but on this day, one was significantly swollen. I managed to find a pharmacy and my request for eye rinse was easily mimed. There was no toilet paper but I did manage to get some eye drops.

Arriving in Cuttack, it was looking like I would survive India. I had good internet for once, and in a relatively good mood with my 15 minutes of free time, I wrote a 'newspaper report' on me, to share with my growing list of Facebook followers:

> *'From Mumbai Times... NICHOLSON BURIES INDIA..... Andrew 'iron guts' Nicholson is making swift progress in his bid to break the Guinness World Circumnavigation Record, attributing his poor personal hygiene to his success. Against his wife's wishes, Nicholson refused to bathe or wash kitchen equipment*

for several months prior to the attempt, to build up immunity. The strategy appears to be working as Nicholson made impressive progress towards Kolkata today. "I've never enjoyed washing" said Nicholson to a packed press conference. "It simply wastes time, hygiene is overrated". Nicholson has ignored all traditional advice on surviving in India; eating whatever, whenever, with no ill effects. "A chicken biryani cooked next to an open sewer simply don't bother me" said Nicholson. Former Olympic teammate Matthew Briggs and coach Lester Pardoe also agreed that Nicholson's lack of cleanliness was a likely contributing factor to his progress. "His stench alone was enough to intimidate any opposition" said the balding Canadian. Meanwhile emergency services are being kept busy in Kolkata in preparation for Nicholson's imminent arrival. ***REUTERS***’

In spite of the ‘all you can eat potato chip and coca cola diet’ I was continuing to lose weight. In a photo taken of me with my shirt off, outside Akshay’s place, it certainly looked like I had been working on the Burma Railway. Arnold and my powerlifting friends would not have been impressed. I was becoming emaciated.

Given the torment of the riding conditions in

India, I started to wonder what it must have been like to work on the Burma Railway as a POW under the Japanese in 1943. In the latter half of the World War, 60,000 Allied soldiers died in horrific conditions during the construction of the Burma Railway.[7] In many respects, my daily workload was similar. I had been working without break for 12-13 hours a day for over two months now, much of it baking in tropical heat and in dangerous conditions. But that was about where the similarities would end. I had chosen this challenge, I was no prisoner. My challenge may have been brutally, hot, hard and dangerous work; but I wasn't going to die of malaria. I wouldn't have fanatical guards standing over me with a bayonet ready to kill me if I were to stop. If I had to, I could stop. I would survive.

I may have endured some less than pleasant and dubiously cooked meals on this journey, but it was more and better than the couple of cups of manky rice the POW's probably got. Dwelling on the horror of such true hardships brought me down to earth. I felt like a wussy and I would complain less...for a while. Our concept of tough has become lost and weak in our western lives of comfort. We have lost the concept of hard. We forget what real hard is, and what our ancestors and forefathers have been through. This trip was bringing me close to an appreciation of what real hardship was and what the real limits of human endurance were.

In spite of the horror, the vast majority of

POW's survived the Burma Railway. Although I grizzled and moaned on the surface, the challenge of trip, however tough, made me appreciate my circumstances. My suffering also couldn't be compared to the cancer sufferers who I was riding for. I certainly pushed myself to an amazing feat and through discomforts that would break most Westerners. But I wasn't forced to, if I chose to, I could make the suffering end.

On my penultimate day in India I stopped at place called Balasore. I renamed it Bellysore, as I felt stomach rumblings. Perhaps Iron Guts Nicholson would not make it out alive after all?

Rolling up to a cheap and dirty hotel, a young friendly porter boy led me to my room. I followed, carefully picking up my bike. "No bikes in room" the officious owner yelled after me. I pressed him for a reason but he just head wobbled.

I threw a tantrum, a public one. I was done with this issue which had been a problem from the start of India. It bugged me and was typical of Indian bureaucracy. "Why not?" I kept pointlessly asking the arrogant boss, who was intent on exerting his authority, just for the sake of it. "Give me a reason? Is it because the bike's not clean enough? What about the room?" "It's the rules" he said, headwobbling. I could hardly figure it was a cleanliness rule as the toilet clearly hadn't been cleaned for months. Bringing my bike into this hotel might've actually made it cleaner. Eventually I had to concede and leave my bike in the unattended garage. The odds of it being there in the morning were even.

I awoke with no further decline in my stomach, Iron Guts had repelled the gurgling. I was half disappointed to see my bike was still in the garage and with no excuse to quit I left Bellysore before sunrise for my final day in India.

The day was little different than any of the previous 16; heat, traffic, pollution. I crossed several palm fringed rivers as I approached the exiting tributaries of the Ganges Delta. I was tempted, as I had been since Mumbai, to cool off in the water; even for just a brief moment. Doing so however would have been foolish, for although millions of locals bathed in these waters, I reminded myself that they also shat in them. The risk of dysentery wasn't worth it, I would just have to sweat.

Approaching Kolkata after more than 200 km, the traffic intensified and I again entered a state of flow similar to Hyderabad. The road to Kolkata passed millions of slums where, for most people, their most valuable possession was a tarpaulin like the one I had bought for $3 the previous evening. For many people it was their most valued possession and served as their house. Mine would be used once to wrap my bike, then dumped in Thailand.

I managed to ride directly to the Silverline hotel Jennie had booked, 5 minutes from the airport. The staff on this occasion were extremely obliging, no problems taking my bike to the room. I took it into the shower and gave it the cleaning it deserved. In spite of the usual deafening traffic, pollution and chaos, the approach had been relatively straightforward and I felt an enormous sense of achievement.

I had done it! I'd beaten India. I had also beaten the Bulgarian cash crises, the Ankara road block, Turkish rain and the resulting collapse of the bottom bracket in Georgia. I had fought wind, heat and mad traffic in India, yet I had still managed some big days.

I was still down on the record but felt I'd gotten over the worst. I remained in the game and had beaten what would be the toughest country to ride in. Yess!!

Racing in India, artist's impression.
By Andrew Nicholson

Chapter 12

South East Asia

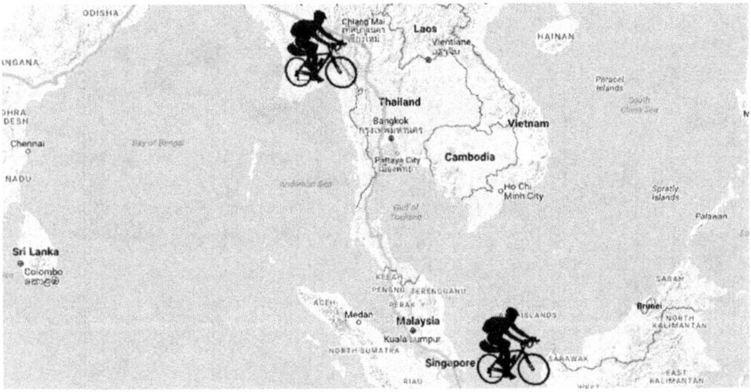

From Kolkata there was to be a short flight to the northern Thai city of Chiang Mai, where Leg 4 would begin. Riding through Myanmar was a bad idea, the only option was over non-sealed jungle roads. I was still on track to fit in the 29,000 km and could afford the short hop.

The world record holder himself, Alan Bate, was living in Thailand; he had received word of my ride and offered to help, but for the moment something had come up. I assumed I would have to continue without help, but word of my ride was starting to spread. Near the end of India I'd put out a plea for help online, and help came from an American named John Graham. John ran bicycle tours in Thailand. He arranged my transfer to Chiang Mai, and had an English-speaking cycle mechanic named Yo meet me and lead me to Mong Cycles for some much needed bike maintenance.

After a quick service, I was on my way south by midday. The heat was as sapping as it had been in India but the air tasted much cleaner. Clear sky and lush jungle hills surrounded the small touristic Thai city. Things felt instantly tidy, clean and organised after the madness of India.

By now I was as far behind the record as I had ever been. I had lost a day in the transfer from India and my required average was now nearing 280 km. Keen to peg back the average, I was frustrated to have to call it a day at Lampang after only 100 km. It was a tough call but there was an isolated gap beyond Lampang and I was too tired to risk riding through the night. Hauling ass would have to start tomorrow. I readied the gear and food, popped an extra half pill, and was asleep by 7:00pm. What felt like seconds later I was riding in the middle of the night through the Thai countryside. By 4:00am I was already racing.

I had gotten over the worst and had beaten the toughest country. Support was waiting in Perth. I was feeling confident as I rode through extreme humidity in the lush northern Thai jungle. I hadn't got behind due to fatigue, just a series of logistical hassles. I could still do this thing but huge days were needed. The roads were lightning fast, there was plenty of shoulder but a strong southerly was negating this advantage.

The 7-11 convenience store chains in Thailand were everywhere and as the name suggests, very convenient. Especially for a cycle tourist, fully stocked with a variety of nutritious and safe food, their greatest appeal was the air conditioning. I'd linger around the fizzy drink machines scooping up small bags of ice which would be tucked behind my neck to fight the heat. It was hard to walk out of the stores but the clock was always running.

I also started to acquire better fruits than could be found in India. Lychees and rambutans would be bungeed onto the aero bars which I would peal and pick as I cycled south. The roads were perfect, and after India the traffic was predictable. On my second day in Thailand I rode a record 397 km all the way to Nakhon Sawan, despite the headwind. During the evening maintenance time in cheap hotels I would gorge myself on mangoes and the fantastic Thai Curries which were readily available. I could feel my immune system respond in appreciation, absorbing the desperately needed nutrients it had been so deprived of in India.

Using a cheap and tiny smartphone in the most comfortable of conditions is less than ideal, but the super small screen combined with an increasing state of fatigue and shaky hands made for time consuming operation. Slow and clumsy on my smartphone, the average 12 year old would thrash me in a texting test. In hindsight I should have made a better choice and paid more attention to the various functions my phone provided before departure. Being resistant to change, Eftpos cards, email and smartphones were all fads that I had hoped would disappear. The chances of the phone being ruined by moisture were high, keeping it dry was difficult enough in normal conditions but near impossible in the upsized torrential downpours I would soon experience.

Lengthy days meant more effort to maintain a charged battery. It required constant fiddling and adjusting of the brightness settings, to avoid running the battery flat. In hindsight, this cheap $40 phone was a poor choice of communication, but now it had to be protected at all costs. It was my lifeline. I had made a rule that it, and only it, had reserved rights to the rear right pocket. Lose the phone and I would lose contact with home, vital information and navigation. If I lost my phone, I was screwed.

I would ride 1,000 km over three days through Northern Thailand. The days were massive. The required total could be soul destroying, depending on how I viewed my progress. I would constantly remind myself that as long as I was moving I was getting closer. One pedal stroke at a time. Breaking down the day into smaller chunks was essential. Around the 100 km mark was an important time to kid myself that the day would be easy. Assuming I had started early, 100 km may have been covered as early as 8am, which would typically mean still 160 km to go. I would take the mind-set that now all I had to do was a 160 km day. How I viewed the required distance played a huge part in increasing moral. Taking on a 'glass half full' approach was essential.

I tried to enjoy the travel experience when conditions were good. There were still moments to reflect on life and the places I was riding through. Tourism is massive in Thailand, there are attractions over the full length of the country. I was constantly passing signs for things I would never have time for; elephant sanctuaries, waterfalls and beaches were posted, always just a couple of kilometres off the main road. Tempting as they were, there simply wasn't time. I was needing to spend up to 16 hours a day peddling. Quite a contrast to the average tourists Thailand experiences. People were friendly; orange robed monks smiled and would return my wave as I headed south, passing Buddha statues, temples and later, paddy fields.

Despite my fatigued physical and mental state, it occurred to me that throughout the trip I hadn't lost anything of importance. I had also managed to maintain accurate records of my ride with diligent and careful use of my spot tracker and cycle computer. I put all this down to my pre-mounting mantra: S.P.C.B.

Before I would mount my bike, I would repeat my mantra S.P.C.B. (*Special Protection against Cruelty to Bicyclists)* Firstly, S for Spot Tracker. Make sure it is working, for without it working, there is no record. P is for Phone, is it safely secured in the right rear pocket? C was for computer, make sure the bike computer is going, the computer was essential as back up evidence. For a couple of days in India, Spot coverage had been almost non-existent and I would need to depend on the evidence of my bike computer. Finally, B for belongings, do I have my backpack and are the contents secure? Belongings meant passport, money and bank cards. In many respects I am a somewhat disorganised person but when it came to things that really mattered, I had a system. The simple mantra worked perfectly. My phone was never dropped, and when I knew it was going to be a navigation nightmare I used trusty duct tape and mounted it onto the aero bars. If I saw anything worth taking a photo of, it was too bad. It wasn't worth unfastening it. Survival and speed came before pretty pictures.

On my fifth day in Thailand I met John Graham. He had messaged me saying he would meet me in the small town of Hua Hin as I passed through. It was about the size of Christchurch. He had been tracking me and he waved me down, along with his one-legged Australian friend and Vietnam veteran named Laurie, outside a modern looking bike shop.

Laurie was soon to set out on his own epic cycle tour. He had plans to bike from Vietnam to Australia to raise awareness of the 50th anniversary of the Australian Task Force's involvement in the Vietnam War. He was looking to raise funds for Australian wounded veterans. Specifically, those who don't get government assistance for post-traumatic stress disorder. I had seen the world but not in a way Laurie had. Like the Burma railway survivors, I wasn't that tough. My trip may have been longer and faster than Laurie's; but I had two legs, he had one. Respect.

Laurie knew I was on a budget, he was supportive of my mission, and as a cyclist he understood the sense of urgency of my trip. The glasses I bought from the Serbian equivalent of a Two Dollar Shop had been dropped and scratched, and with my eye infection at its height I needed a new pair. Laurie whipped out his wallet and insisted on paying for a pair. He also bought me a bunch of energy gels before literally pushing me on my way.

The tail end of the monsoon season was still

lingering and as I headed further south the daily downpours were increasing in intensity. Day 92 was to be my last in Thailand; my goal, the Malaysian border. I was around 50 km from the border town of Ban Dan Nok and as usual the heat was draining me. The sun was high and I was grovelling. It was around 3:00pm and I started to look forward to the daily downpour. I just hoped it would be mild, riding safely and managing equipment had been stressful in the recent afternoon downpours. I could see the dark clouds building as they had previously, and braced for the deluge. Important objects like passports, the phone and the diary were secured in several layers of plastic. It was going to hose down.

Suddenly the bomb dropped and my last two hours in Thailand quickly became a swimming race. The heavens didn't just open, they collapsed! I had no idea it was possible for it to rain this hard, the rain was even thicker than the previously extremely thick days. Lightning was striking and exploding within what felt like metres from me. I had never experienced a storm like this in my life! It was sudden, constant and intense. My heart was racing. The water was rising on the roads faster than it could be drained. Tree branches and other debris were being washed toward me. I was forced to cycle at an increasingly slower pace.

Before long the water was up to my bottom bracket and my wheels were carving their way through what had become a fast-flowing river. With the road tapering to the left it became necessary to move to the right to avoid drowning. Moving into the lanes of passing traffic was obviously dangerous but the traffic soon headed for higher ground then came to a stop. Even locals weren't game to drive in this supersized deluge. Visibility became almost nil given the black clouds and torrents from above. This monsoon had arrived late in the day and it was getting dark. I simply had to keep moving. Unable to move quickly, I actually started to get cold? An hour earlier I had been sweltering. My only warm clothes were in a rubbish skip at Tbilisi airport and I wasn't going back. Saving every ounce of space and weight had been essential. I became seriously worried about my chain. I had been using the same chain since Tbilisi and it was becoming increasingly stretched and occasionally creaking or slipping. I could probably fix it if it broke. But if it broke now it would be lost at the bottom of the road and swept into the gutter.

Rain and rage, Thailand

Finally, the town of Ban Dan Nok appeared. I wheeled my bike into a cheap hotel that was usually intended for hourly rental. My passports had stayed dry but the increasingly large bag of receipts I had collected since Mumbai had only been sloppily secured. I would later open a bag of soggy *papier mâché*. They were soaked through, and many were illegible, nothing could be done. I had lost some valuable back up evidence for the record, but I had survived yet another testing day. I found food, failed to dry anything and collapsed.

In wet clothes, I crossed the Thai Malaysia border at 6:00am without incident. The smooth tar sealed road continued but the 'tantrum metre' was soon set to reach extreme. Today's stressor would be traffic lights.

Malaysians love traffic lights, they put them everywhere, even in random places where there is little traffic. They even seem to enjoy waiting. Scooting around them doesn't work. The semi illegal tactic of turning left, doing a U-turn, then turning left again is impossible. A raised up traffic island would usually require dismounting and remounting. I just had to wait, time and time again, as I headed through the populated coastal areas, down through Butterworth and Port Dickinson. This was a tight bike race with a world record in sight and I was being held up by traffic lights. I threw several tantrums.

Bypassing the main highway, I found a 50 km stretch of stunning coastal section on the way to Malacca. An idyllic, flat and single lane road, with beach and palm trees on my right and lush forest on my left. Approaching me was what looked like a scruffy European cycle tourist, on what appeared to be a BMX? Sure enough, laden with double panniers front and rear, came Calum Mackintosh. Not Scottish, but Australian.

Calum had started in Melbourne and was attempting to circumnavigate the world on a BMX! Dude, seriously? I was three months into my journey and three quarters done. Callum had been going a little over a year and was a quarter of the way around the world. He was taking his time and from his tales of pushing his bike over muddy trails in Sumatra I'm guessing he wasn't exactly taking the easiest or most direct route. Much respect.

In spite of having to ride all day I had still encountered other touring cyclists with awesome goals and big travel stories. I met James in Georgia who was taking three years to ride the planet and was about to ride through a Russian Winter. I met Andrew and Amanda in Canmore who were taking three years to travel the length of the Americas. A Warm Showers French family I met in Nancy had just ridden with three children down South America. I had now met Callum who was riding a BMX around the planet. All were inspirational. I was unlikely to ever race around the planet again but they inspired me to do more sensibly paced cycle touring with Marcela in the future.

Callum Mackintosh, cycling the world by BMX (Malaysia)

On Day 91 I exited Malaysia from the massive city of Johor Bahru and entered my 23rd country, Singapore, where the rubbish had suddenly vanished. The threats of beatings has had the desired effect. I had about six hours before my flight and wasted 40 min getting lost in an area around a race course. I got in but couldn't get out and threw a tantrum.

Eventually I headed downtown where for a moment I showed a rare sign of complacency. Trying to ride and navigate at the same time, I looked up too late. I had made a date with the rear of a taxi, and I wasn't getting out! Shoulder charging the boot I toppled back to the pavement. The irate taxi driver quickly hopped out to survey for any damage to his vehicle.

"You wait! You wait here!" he yelled at me accusingly. I immediately apologised, conceding that the collision was entirely my fault. I checked my own machine, and more importantly my body, for damage. I had seriously bruised my shoulder which had taken the brunt of the collision, but otherwise I was okay.

The taxi driver showed zero concern for my wellbeing and continued thoroughly inspecting his taxi for the slightest damage. All I'd left was a sweaty imprint of my shoulder. "You wait, you wait, I call police!" He kept yelling while inspecting further, finding nothing, while I nursed my shoulder. "In Singapore we follow law" he yelled.

Satisfied there was no damage he slammed his door, gave me a hate look and went back to business. In New Zealand, we give shit when others are hurt, I thought. Wanker.

I rolled up to a bike shop a few kilometres from the airport and was met by none other than the madman who held the world record for cycling around the world by bike, Alan Bate. Alan had come down from his home in Thailand to both meet me and support me, and was waiting for me at a bike shop. Alan is an intense individual who confessed that his attempt had nearly broken him both physically and emotionally. He showed excellent sportsmanship by organising a bike service for me and stuffing me full of food, before escorting me to the airport. I felt like I had known him for years. He was a crazy but driven character. You had to be, to take on this type of challenge.

By now I had now cycled 20,994 kilometres. It wasn't until I boarded the plane that I realised I was about to see my beautiful wife! Fantastically, thanks to a contribution from my Dad, it had been arranged that Marcela could meet me in Perth and support me across the Nullarbor Plain from a campervan. We would have nine days before Marcela needed to return the van in Adelaide and head back to work.

Since leaving my family in the Czech Republic I had desperately held onto the thought that, if I could make it to Perth and meet Marcela, and be at least roughly on schedule, then I could make it all the way. Her support would surely get me through. From Perth onward there would be no more cultural challenges and I would get a small break from logistics, all the thinking and organisation would be taken care of. Perth therefore became my mental finish line. In reality I still had nearly a third of the journey to cover, and I needed to cover it fast if I was to catch up on the record. For nine days, however, I would have support of the best kind. And if I made the most of those nine days then I would be a relative stone's throw from the actual finish line.

Chapter 13

Australia

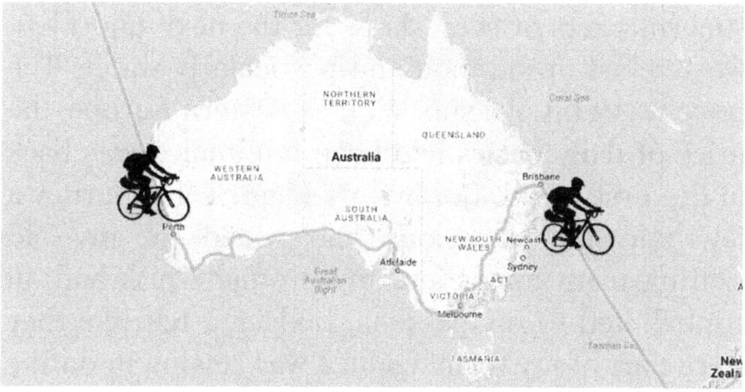

I hadn't seen Marcela for three months now and after a long and emotional embrace, we went immediately into race mode. The clock was always ticking. I had enlisted the help of a certain Frank Anderson for our exit from Perth. Frank was another kind and supportive link from old speed skating days. Passionate about the sport and a tough Master's competitor, Frank held the Perth speed skating club together. A big ask in sports mad Australia, we had already passed countless AFL and Rugby fields, swimming pools and cricket grounds. Perth has one ice rink and speed skating has to share it with the public and other ice sports.

Frank guided me to AvantiPlus for some more bike repairs while Marcela collected the small 'Wicked' campervan which would be the mothership for the next nine days. Like all my hosts and helpers, it was a shame to say goodbye to Frank after such a short meeting. He understood the sense of urgency and pointed us to the Albany Highway.

Knowing there would be little in the way of supermarkets or even shops for the next 3,500 km, we stocked up on food and particularly water. The price was a bit of a shock. Since Eastern Europe, the price of daily basics had been minimal. I was back in the first world. But by this stage of the journey a few personal donations had rolled in, my old skating team mates and my brother Chris had all contributed to my personal budget. I felt like they were part of my team again. I was closing in on the finish line, too close to care about a few dollars now, but still, there were no luxuries. There was no need for fancy, basics were working. I was still in the race but I had to move!

Marcela began leapfrogging me, stopping to reorganise the van as we headed South on the Albany Highway. Leaving Perth, I immediately encountered heavy coarse chip road. This evil road surface would be with me through to the finish line. I hate the stuff and the majority of New Zealand and Australian roads are constructed with it. It's also known in Australia as blue chip. It grinds and shakes the life from you, especially on a racing bike with high pressure, narrow tyres. The 'saddle area' in particular takes a constant pounding. Coarse chip also leads to coarse language. Relaxing on the bike is impossible, the continuous vibrating through the frame makes it difficult to settle into a comfortable rhythm. As well as energy sapping it is a good 2-4kph slower than smooth tar seal.

Some sections were worse than others, depending how recently the road was sealed and the size of the stones. Traffic itself is intended to help compact and compress the chip, which forms a smoother surface in the natural line of traffic. Cyclists, however, should be riding in the shoulder, where we make little impact and subsequently the surface on the shoulder is horrible. Closer to the centre line the surface improves, but riding there massively increases the chance of becoming instant road kill.

The only time I'd wished for coarse chip was in the rain in Turkey as its only benefit to a cyclist is the draining effect. There was no sign of rain here. It was dry and brutally hot. Parts of the globe, particularly India, Georgia and Eastern Europe, had long sections of pitted, cracked and potholed roads. Annoying, but if picked your line you would at least be on a relatively smooth surface. In Australia or New Zealand you get teased, when you get to ride through towns of perfect tar seal, bringing just a few moments of peace, before re-joining the groin grinding highways.

Shortly before sleep on day 2, Marcela let out a scream which startled all the kangaroos within twenty miles. A spider! Normally I have little tolerance for her pathetic arachnophobic squeals, but this was Australia and spiders could kill you. The squeal-causing spider was big, hairy and looked evil. It freaked me out and I made quick and careful work of dispatching it with the fish slice.

To break the world record I had to cycle a minimum of 29,000 kilometres. Having had to adapt my route due various issues, I was now concerned I might not have enough physical land left to meet this requirement without traveling west. So, being mindful to avoid running out of planet we had needed to take a very indirect route across Western Australia. On Day 3 we would pass through Esperance.

Marcela had driven ahead for ice and water to a settlement called Jerramungup, where a precious 20 minute stop was planned. Entering the highway from a side road, I saw in the distance a heavily laden touring bike, seemingly rider-less. As I got closer a person emerged from under the huge piles of gear. We stopped to chat and a tiny young French girl named Veronica introduced herself. Cycle tourists were rare out here, and at about five feet tall Veronica could have been no more than 20. She was travelling completely alone and had taken

14 days to get here from Perth (it had taken me three). At first look it seemed Veronica was prepared. She had quality clothing, a great bike and ample expensive looking camping gear. But when I asked her if she had enough water, she shook both her head and her bottle, indicating only a few sips. Jerramungup was still 30 km east and into a head wind. With a grossly overloaded touring bike it would have taken her two hours and it was hot! It's no surprise tourists die in the outback. I spared what I could and after a break Marcela went back to check on her.

I left Marcela to stock up on supplies in Esperance and felt a sting shortly after I put my helmet on - a spider in my helmet, perhaps? I felt it swell and itch for the rest of the day. As I cycled away from Esperance I noticed some strange clouds in the distance. These, I later found out, were smoke. We camped that night, unaware of the raging bush fires further south that had claimed the lives of four people. We would later realise that we had entered the highway only a couple of hours before it was closed.

It was forecast to be hot, extremely hot, over 40°Celsius. I had never experienced extreme hot, let alone ride a bike 300 km each day through it. Extreme cold, yes, the ice skating thing. In 1987 the British Columbia Outdoor Champs were held in Dawson Creek, Northern British Columbia. It dropped to minus 30°C before officials finally cancelled the competition. With wind chill it felt like any exposed body part was being cut with a knife. With so many extreme winters I have become comfortable in cold environments, Dunedin is positively tropical compared to some of the places I called home as a speed skater. Extreme cold might cut to the bone but you can dress and prepare for it. I was about to discover that extreme heat cooks, and there would be no escaping it.

The 5:00am alarm woke me with a jolt. I gave Marcela a kiss, and already in my cycling gear, I rolled out the van door and stepped onto the bike. Every detail had been organised for an instant start. I just had to adjust my helmet to fit my Frankenstein look. My head was still swollen from the unidentified insect bite.

"Bye, baby", I'd gently close the van door and by 5:05am I was rolling along at 25kph, still half asleep. Marcela would lie in for another 30 minutes, then start coffee and breakfast. Around 7:30am the Wicked horn would sound, Marcela would pass and then be waiting ahead with the usual - a porridge bomb and fresh coffee. I would grab it on the move, no time for stopping. Another huge day was planned and it was already sweltering. Later that morning we would reach Norseman. The last town for 1,000 km. We had made the usual efficient start and covered 100 km, but with over 200 km to go, we were in for a stonker!!

In Norseman we found a pharmacy and got some antihistamines for my swollen head. They seemed to have an immediate effect. No other dangerous symptoms had developed. The trip wouldn't end with spider death, after all. It was probably just a bee.

I left Marcela in Norseman to do the shopping, fill up the van and other duties. The next town wasn't until in Ceduna; 1,500 km east. I plodded off in the increasing heat with a strong side wind, hoping it would swing to a tail wind, as forecast.

By midday the temperature had topped 43 degrees Celsius. It was drying me out and draining me fast. India and Thailand made me sweat but

Australia was cooking me. Everything was so dry. Experiencing both heat and wind first-hand, I could easily get a clear understanding of how phenomenally fast Australia's deadly bushfires can travel. There was no moisture in the air. This was dry, hot desert, typical of most of Australia. I had left Norseman with nearly two litres of water, but within an hour I was running low with still no sign of Marcela. This was the type of heat that could kill you quickly, but I wouldn't die out here. Since Norseman I had joined the Eyre highway. It is the main link across Australia and traffic was passing frequently. Help was at hand. Going off the main highways in Australia is a different story and I seriously hoped Veronica wouldn't try.

The black alloy aerobars became too hot to hold. I became concerned about tyre pressure, and the brakes would scream at the slightest touch. Even if I had time to stop, the sun was high and there was no shade. I wondered, what was taking Marcela so long back in Norseman? We'd seen the attractions, a corrugated iron statue of a camel and a tailings dump from the gold mining past. Marcela had to have screwed up. I couldn't get heat stroke, dehydrated or die out here, so it seemed I would just have to be embarrassingly rescued by a passing vehicle. I started to look for the first, which would probably be of the tattooed-trucker-named-Stevo type, behind the wheel of one of the massive road trains. I'd get a lecture and complete with cab footage I'd make it onto 'Outback Truckers'. I'd be made to look an idiot...*"Next on Outback Truckers...a Kiwi tries to ride the Nullarbor without water..."*

The highway became even straighter and flatter, you could see the approaching traffic for miles. The next vehicle took forever to arrive and fortunately it turned out to be the mother ship. Marcela had simply been faffing about, I gave her a growling and immediately swapped my bike jersey for another that had been soaked in ice. It would dry within ten minutes and we would repeat the process all day. I'd also collect a crushed ice bag and tuck it behind my neck, into my jersey where it would also drip dry within minutes. We would try to stop to reorder things and eat, but became concerned about overheating the vehicle, as the aircon simply had to stay on. The flies became thicker. It was impossible to escape them. Opening the door for even five seconds meant dozens would follow you in and invade. 20 seconds and you'd have hundreds. Stopping was pointless.

The forecast tail wind eventuated, but in the conditions I was drained and unable to turn it into any significant gain. We were going through litres and litres of water. Drinking it was the priority, then came cooling. Washing was well down the order!! A huge chunk of our budget was spent on water and ice. Without support, for me to have managed these distances alone would have been impossible. Australia was hot, dry and empty. Without Marcela and a campervan, the record would have been gone. We could afford only a few days with support on my whole trip and we certainly choose it wisely. I thought about Mark Beaumont's record and how he rode this section alone. Serious manly points. Australia was a killer.

The flies increased as we approached Balladonia which I assumed was their capital. "Nah mate, they're all right", commented the proprietor of the isolated road house. "They only wanna crawl in ya mouth, up ya nose and in yer ears", as if it were nothing. You don't dare open your mouth for fear of swallowing at least half a dozen. The flies were bigger and more persistent than wussy Kiwi flies and they can't be outpaced. Even at 40kph they get sucked along in your slipstream and manage to blanket you.

We had seen people using the black hair net covers and anticipating this, Marcela had sensibly bought one. It was highly irritating for cycling but becoming necessary. I rode along looking like a widow at a funeral. I would frequently forget to lift the netting before drinking or eating, stuffing a mouthful of hair net in my gob. A split second to raise it to eat or drink usually meant several flies would get trapped inside. There was no escaping them.

The flies kept us moving, and when the sun finally went down and the temperature dropped below 30°C again, I started to breathe. Eventually it even cooled enough for the flies to call it a day. In a bright orange outback sunset, we approached the famous 90 mile straight, the longest in Australia. 146 kilometres without a single bend.

The vast, treeless and mesmerising Nullarbor

Plain has a powerful impact. Whatever your direction, the scale of the scenery is massive. Wooded hills flatten into a bluebush-studded plateau, and mobs of kangaroos line the road. Signs of human habitations are rare, with the occasional vast cattle station evident every 100 km or so. Crossing the Nullarbor by car would seem like an adventure for some, but by bicycle you would have to be mad. And trying to cover over 300 km per day means you would have to be insane. But compared to the first crossing by Europeans, I was a wussy.

The Aboriginal name for the Nullarbor Plain is Oondiri, meaning 'the waterless'. This is apt as the average annual rainfall for the area is around 184.1mm. Edward Eyre, together with his Aboriginal companion Wylie, was the first European to traverse the coastline of the Great Australian Bight and the Nullarbor Plain by land in 1840-1841, on an almost 2000 mile trip to Albany, Western Australia. He had originally led the expedition with John Baxter and three aborigines. On 29 April 1841 two of the aborigines killed Baxter and left with most of the supplies, and Eyre and Wylie were only able to survive because they chanced to encounter, at a bay near Esperance, a French whaling ship.[8] They earned some serious manly points from the NGF and I felt like I was cheating by having support.

Traveling with support continued to be relatively easy in spite of the heat. I was clocking up huge days and pegging back the required average.

"Urrgg" meant I wanted food. "Urrgh Urrgh" meant ice...after a grunt and point, five minutes later Marcela would be standing at the side of the road with my demand. A readymade squeezy-bag of porridge, a sandwich, fruit bits, or an ice bag. We didn't need to be sponsored by 'Easy Bar', supermarket basics were working just fine. We were glad we had stocked up in Norseman, the cost of basic groceries at the roadhouses was outrageous. Outside the Nullarbor Roadhouse a bike is exhibited as the first bike to be cycled across Australia by a helmeted rider. It looks like a chopper.

Navigation consisted of leaving the road and turning left for the day. Even with head winds, progress was great. I simply had to ride; there was no route planning, no washing clothes or food foraging. I could fall over wherever I liked and the roadside stops were evenly spaced. The biggest morale booster was seeing Marcela, albeit briefly, throughout the day. I may have still had to ride over 300 km per day, but compared to what I had been through, it was a holiday.

I'd been right to use Perth as the mental finish line. With Marcela's support I knew I could get quickly to Adelaide, and from there I would be almost home and nothing would stop me. A bigger budget would certainly have got me around the planet much faster. The difference between supported and unsupported is huge! I hope that out of respect to riders who are silly enough to attempt this challenge, a distinction can be made. Time will tell. Records progress. Meanwhile, Marcela had helped to get me within range of Port Augusta and I was now close to civilisation.

Over eight days I had averaged 330 km a day but the support had come to an end. Marcela and I woke at 3:50am with everything prepared for an instant start. She would now leave me and drive 500 km to Adelaide, return the van, and fly back home to work. I would need to make my way across the last of the outback alone and head for Port Augusta. The night before we said proper goodbyes, and agreed on a sensible, quick and emotion free departure. She had a plane to catch and I had a record to break. Within ten minutes of the 3:50am alarm, we had parted. My rock was gone and I was on my own again and I was by no means done. I had crossed the most isolated section at speed but I may have come close to emptying the tank. Only 4,000 km to go, but my strength was seriously depleted. The fatigue had become long term, and something was likely to break. The charge across the Nullabor had drained the last of my energy. I was becoming weak.

I hadn't had to carry anything since Perth and I immediately felt the significance of the weight of my pack on my bike. Within a few pedal strokes yet another seat post bolt snapped. Clearly this bolt on a racing bike was not designed for the extra weight.

I was on my own at 4:00am in the outback, 200 km from a town. I plodded slowly onwards for the day. Starting out, I was weighed down with eight litres of water, plus gear. The obvious predominant southerly wind picked up as I turned south toward the town of Port Augusta.

I'd been on the road all day and it felt strange to be in a proper town. I gorged myself on two pies before heading off to a Warm Showers host in a town of Wilmington, nestled near the stunning Flinders ranges. I felt like company after the isolation and I would find it in a kind couple named Simon and Heather.

Heather was the third cancer survivor I stayed with and had recently had chemo. Like Paco in

Spain, she showed no visible signs of struggle. Again it was a timely reminder of the cause behind my ride, also a reminder of the relevance of my own suffering. Simon and Heather got up early to have breakfast with me, shoved some sandwiches in my pockets and encouraged me onwards. It didn't take long for the wind to pick up; I was in for one slow day.

Both traffic and wind increased as I joined the main Stuart Highway to Adelaide. The frequency of towns and petrol stations increased, as did size of the chip. It was a struggle from the start. Head down, I was sitting at barely 20 kph. The day dragged on and on.

Given that 320 km needed to be covered, it was 10:00pm by the time I reached Adelaide. The hostel was crowded with various nationalities but I was somehow lucky to get an empty room. I was losing enthusiasm and feeling terribly sorry for myself, until I thought of Heather. I couldn't stop now.

I didn't bother keeping quiet as I wheeled my bike down the hostel hallway at 5:00am. Some of the party backpacker types were still up and making it known to all. I was so grateful to have scored a room to myself, away from the communal areas. I felt weaker than ever, following the tougher than usual beating I had received the previous day.

The sun was rising early, but I had already made progress south. The baking temperatures I had experienced in Western Australia were no longer forecast, only a mild 30 degrees was expected. I negotiated my way through the city centre and toward the eastern suburbs in the Adelaide hills, where I knew I was in for a climb.

After the outback it felt weird to be riding through city streets again. The tidy green suburbs on the outskirts reminded me of Christchurch, an appropriate sister city. The sense of familiarity assured me I was getting closer to home. After all, I'd nearly cycled a lap. A lap of the planet!

Generally, I lost perspective of the whole circumnavigation thing. My mind had been focused on getting through one day at a time. I'd just been trying to get as far east as possible, surviving bit by bit. Now I was getting close. It occurred to me that technically, I had now already circumnavigated the planet.

In 1986 on a skating trip, some kind Australian skaters gave me a lift from Adelaide to Melbourne. I had been here before and come from the opposite direction. I had circumnavigated the planet.

The first person to circumnavigate the planet by any means is usually considered to be Ferdinand Magellan (Fernão de Magalhães).[9] Magellan intended to have a successful journey when his expedition set off from Spain on 20 September 1519, but things were a mess right from the start. Five ships left Spain, but only three made it to the Pacific Ocean. One of the ships was lost in an attempted mutiny when the expedition was sailing along South America; another deserted when they were sailing through what is now known as the Strait of Magellan. After three months across the Pacific without obtaining provisions his crew were reduced to eating rats. Starvation took hold and 17 died before he made landfall in what is today Guam. Magellan then thought it a great idea to get involved with a local war in the Philippines. The battle of Mactan was poorly planned by the overly confident Magellan. He ended up face down in the tropical shallows with a bamboo lance through him. The voyage continued west under the command of a man named Juan Sebastian Elcano. A further ship was leaking and abandoned while another captured. The now lone Victoria and her diminished crew went back on the rat diet, crossing the Indian Ocean. Many more died of scurvy and disease took its toll during this desperate leg homewards. Along the African coast they were briefly captured by their Portuguese enemies before narrowly escaping (minus a few mates they abandoned to the Portuguese). After nearly four years Elcano limped back to Spain with 17 survivors and one ship. Manly points galore but still not the first circumnavigation.

The real honour of 'first circumnavigation'

should surely go to Magellan's personal slave, Enrique of Malacca. Enrique had been at Magellan's side since around 1511, when Magellan took him as a spoil of war in the East Indies and promptly re-named him Enrique from whatever his original name was. (This has been lost to history.) Enrique scarpered after the battle of Mactan and whether or not he made it the last few hundred kilometres back to Malacca is unknown. Close enough I say. Enrique gets my vote, and going by those rules I realised in Adelaide that I had circumnavigated the planet. Nearly all of it by bicycle.

My own circumnavigation was also starting to look awkward. The navigation over the Adelaide hills looked confusing and I was trashed before the day had even begun. After more than three months, I was finally slowing down. The main highway was forbidden for cyclists and there was no clear secondary road. Still, at least I didn't scurvy or have to eat rats for breakfast. I had a squashed cake, left over from Port Augusta.

With the sun still below the horizon, dozens of serious looking riders were on the streets of Adelaide for early morning training. Adelaide has become a hotbed for Australian cycling. The Tour Down Under and the annual Festival of Cycling have no doubt contributed to the busy and competitive local cycling scene. The bike shops will be loving it, with fashion cyclists and MAMILs (middle aged men in lycra) all keenly spending up on magazines, pro team jerseys and numerous 'must have' items.

Still unsure of the best route out of Adelaide, I stopped to ask a small group of cool riders on million dollar machines. It seemed that some sort of unofficial race up the main climb was about to begin. I checked my bearings with a guy wearing $800 sunglasses. He glanced at me briefly and rudely shooed me forward, hoping his cool mates wouldn't see him hanging out with the scruffy old cycle tourist wearing his bib over his jersey.

It was obvious by now that I no longer resembled a racing cyclist. Looking down at my hairy legs, big pack and the 23 things stuck to my filthy bike with sellotape, I realised I did not belong here. Mr Cool's group reminded me of when I raced as a kid. Posers, in the sport for the culture, gear and toys, rather than for the love of cycling. Alone, with the sun now rising, I began the long climb out of Adelaide at a plod.

My world ride and skating dream were largely possible because I had learned to do without, to prioritise and sacrifice cool for practical. I could either be fast, or look fast. There wasn't the money for both. Sacrificing cool for practical had often left me isolated. I'd been used to that.

When I first took up bike racing I became an easy target for cycling bullies. Being physically small and appearing in all manner of garbage equipment, I spoilt their cool image of cycling. Being able to hold my own on a bike with the cool gang certainly didn't help my popularity. Unable to beat Chris in cycling, it was easier for cycling bullies to take it out on his weedy little brother. "Did you get that wheel from a rubbish dump?" I was once asked by a younger version of Mr Cool. He was not far off the mark, I had in fact found it at a road side collection, but it meant I saved a few extra dollars for a plane ticket.

About this time I had entered high school totally disinterested. I hung out with a small bunch of kids from my Intermediate School for the first year, but by Fourth Form the order of cool had been firmly established and I had failed to make the grades. I blame my Charlie Brown shoes. Even with a dress code there was still room for a fashion show in the school grounds. Ways to differentiate between the fashionably hip and the highly uncool. In the '80s a whole caste system evolved around the shoe. If you were cool you had Nomads, you were somebody. Treks were a cheaper second grade alternative, acceptable, but only just.

I was still wearing Charlie Browns, a primary school Warehouse equivalent. An uncool shoe with an even more uncool name. I became an untouchable. The only other option was Roman sandals. The few who had chosen to wear Roman sandals on day one had since become teenage suicide statistics. Charlie Brown wearers were now the lowest. We were not accepted into cool groups. We would have to look elsewhere for our place in the school. Kids can be cruel.

Being banished from cool groups I joined whatever group was left, mine was an odd combination of misfits and rejects. There were nerdy Norbert Poindexters in the group who also wore Charlie Browns. Beavis and Butthead were there as was a Bart Simpson type. There was also an Eric Cartman lookalike named Barry who wore stolen Nomads.

Vandalism and arson were favourite pastimes in this group. Back when you could still buy dangerous fireworks, Guy Fawkes time was the highlight of the year. The Poindexters saw the fire play as scientific experiments, the rest of us just loved blowing stuff up. I enjoyed blowing things up too but I didn't fit any of the subcategories in the group. But like most kids, I just needed to feel part of something. I guess I became a member by default.

Barry was an expert shoplifter. We would bus into Queen Street where he would steal an assortment of junk, which we would either lose or blow up. I never joined in the actual crimes. I like to think I was too honest rather than too scared to join in the actual lifting. But I started to worry that one day there was a good chance I'd end up becoming Barry's bitch in jail. Barry and his mates were a laugh but they were losers. I'd be better off alone at school breaks, even then I recognised that you become the sum of those you hang around with. At school I became a complete loner. My Charlie Brown's prevented me from joining other groups.

However uncool, I appreciated that my Charlie Browns were practical for the few hours of school work. They did the job and I never resented my parents for making me wear them. Dad had made it clear that if I could do without a few things then perhaps he would top up what I couldn't save for the next year's Aussie skating champs. I was happy with the deal; they were just shoes? Winning the champs meant more to me then looking cool.

I didn't care if I looked cool leaving Adelaide either. I had another race to win. A few minutes into the climb out of Adelaide, Mr Cool and his peloton appeared on the switchback below me, their race had begun. I went into ego drive; I would win the climb in a solo breakaway. I had won the unofficial race into Madison, but that was nearly three months ago, yet, I still had speed, surely? Mr Cool would be thrashed by a dirty old cycle tourist with a pack.

I got off the seat and began to kick. Nothing happened and few seconds later Mr Cool and his gang swamped me and said, “hmmft” as they passed. I was finally getting long term tired. My body was losing its strength.

My brain was also working slower and navigation by secondary routes was awkward. The roads I ended up on weren’t even roughly parallel with the main highway. I battled over several steep gravel roads. The tantrums upsized. It was a mess and it took me all morning to get to Murray Bridge, which as the crow flies, was only 70 km from where I started in Adelaide. I’d only done just over 100 km in horrible conditions and I was pissed. It was a navigation tantrum really. I texted Jennie that I wished I’d get hit by a car, later feeling bad about it. I slogged on, to the small town of Keith, the next day heading south toward Dartmoor.

Yet another fantastic Warm Showers host named Michael came out to meet me. Michael got on the phone the moment we arrived, and organised free accommodation for the following day at Port Campbell. The ride along the Great Ocean Road providing stunning views over the Southern Ocean.

There was a cold southerly blowing when I left the Port Campbell Hostel at 6:00am. I had dumped most of my warm clothes long ago, and within minutes I was soaked and shivering. I passed the Twelve Apostles and headed towards Geelong and the Queenscliff Ferry. Australia had produced the most brutally hot temperatures so far on the trip, but on this day it had produced the coldest. I was freezing and rummaged through a rubbish bin to find extra insulation.

I made my way into Melbourne and north toward the suburb of Dandenong where I would stay with my brother Paul, the founder of the inaugural Nicholson Grovel Ride Record. He drove out to meet me and guided me to his home, later commenting that I looked just like someone riding home from work.

It was great to catch up with Paul and he proved the perfect crew, tending to my every need, while we moaned to each other about modern teaching. In the morning I pushed my departure time forward to an unheard of late start of 7:30am. I really wanted to make the most of catching up with Paul and his family, including my four half-Vietnamese nephews.

The Battle out of Melbourne was a draw, there were a few nasty hills and traffic reminiscent of the big American cities but I made acceptable progress. It was Saturday, apparently. Cricket games were being played in comfortable temperatures in quiet country towns, north of the city. On a peaceful country road about 60 km from the town of Shepparton I showed a rare sign of complacency.

Generally, I avoid sticking things in the front

wheel while I ride. I handle plastic bags, jerseys or arm warmers carefully, keeping items clear of the spokes. On this occasion, I slung my CamelBak pack off my shoulder to get at a cookie. The buckle caught in the spokes and pulled the whole pack into the front wheel. The wheel immediately stopped and I didn't. Not a fast crash, but a nasty one. Rather than a tumble and slide, I felt like I'd been power slammed by Hulk Hogan. I was hurt but I didn't feel any broken limbs. My ribs were seriously bruised and I'd suffered a few cuts. I had the energy to throw a tantrum which was good sign.

There was bike damage. I put the tantrum aside and focused on the issue. At first glance I noticed what appeared to be a broken spoke. On closer inspection I realised that the problem went beyond basic bike first aid. I had received another road block.

The spoke hadn't just broken; it had ripped the nipple right through the rim. I needed a new wheel. Spinning the wheel, the buckled rim immediately sank into the brake pad. I completely released the cable to the front brake and the wheel spun with the smallest of clearance possible without hitting the forks. The buckle was at its maximum. If I avoided bumps, let some air out of the front tyre and kept my weight on the seat; it might hold out for a while. Eventually a second spoke break would lead to a complete collapse.

Howard and Diana from Warm Showers were

to be my saviours that night. Howard rode out to meet a racing cyclist, but found a bloodied and broken tourist with a wonky wheel. Howard was a keen local rider and promptly tracked down the owner of the AvantiPlus store in Shepparton. Trevor from AvantiPlus met me at 9:00am the next morning as promised. It looked like I had inconvenienced the jolly enthusiast, but he supported my cause, gave me a wheel that would do the job at no cost, and sent me on my way. The wheel collapse could have happened in far worse circumstances.

In spite of a good tailwind and the short 160 km to Albury, I suffered massively on Day 106. The crash had left me beaten up, my ribs ached and finding a comfortable position on the bike was impossible. On top this I had developed a nasty stomach bug which killed my appetite. I knew I needed to eat, but I simply couldn't. I'd done my time, I just wanted this trip done. A nail went through my tyre and yet another seat bolt broke. I tried to stop and lie down on benches at roadside stops, but the flies made rest impossible. Dianne and Howard, who cared for me in Shepparton, had arranged for a friend of theirs to host me for a night. I trudged on to Jude's place and she also tried to nurse me to health. A fourth tough cancer battler. Uncanny.

Unlike the endless 3,000 km crossing from Perth to Adelaide, there were a few actual towns on the Newell highway which runs directly through inland Victoria, New South Wales and eventually into Queensland.

For a tiring cyclist, however, the towns are still few and far between. It was essential to stick to the main highway and by now it was into December and getting hot! Riding in temperatures that were well over 30°C, I had to take care to fill up on water between towns. On Day 108 the wind continued to hate me for all of the 308 km to the insignificant town of West Wyalong.

It was a grovel of a day and by the time I plodded up to the Royal Hotel I was spent. These no frills, small town Aussie pub/hotels were ideal, given my low budget and the need for a simple meal and bed. I entered the busy establishment a couple of hours past knock off time, just as the singlets of the beer gutted locals were becoming increasingly drenched in spittle and Fosters. Fat gutted league experts became wiser as the game continued and the beer got guzzled. I probably smelled no better than the typical patron but, still in my cycling gear, I clearly stood out from the crowd.

Heads turned as I shuffled past the pokies and bellies, making my way to the bar which doubled as the hotel reception. Somewhere in the slurred conversations coming from the footy and trucking experts I heard the words "leg shaving pussy". I was in a foul mood after a torturous day, turning angrily to locate the insult. Unable to pinpoint the correct belly I sensibly let it rest.

Drunk beer-bellied ocker versus emaciated cyclist would have made for an amusing Aussie bar brawl, but it wasn't worth it. Sheila at the bar would have beaten the snot out of me in my current state. Pussy? Right, I was a real pussy, I'd only ridden solo around 90 percent of the planet in 100 days, not like the tough Aussies in this establishment. As for the leg shaving bit, I didn't bother, aerodynamics is only important at speed and there was no speed at this stage of the journey. It had become a slow and torturous plod, from dawn to dusk. Not in the mood to discuss trucking or NRL, I took the meal on offer in my room, and after the standard reorganisation I fell into an instant slumber. Day done.

The forecast for the following day was for heat and headwinds. They got it right. Within two hours I was both battling a nasty headwind and cooking in the sun, making slow progress towards the town of Forbes and then Parkes. I took a reasonable break with a dip in the Parkes' community swimming pool and did my best to reduce my temperature, reluctant to continue. But the record was too close now, I couldn't hang around pools.

I plodded on toward Dubbo, finding that I was overheating again within 10 minutes, with my average dropping. I arrived late in Dubbo, and stocked up at Woolworths before finding out that Jennie had already arranged a meal for me. For once I had more food then I could carry or eat the next morning.

In spite of the thousands of calories I was consuming each day, I was looking increasingly gaunt. Even at the start of the day my cheek bones were showing, and my face was burned and weather beaten. The buffer on the record was still small. I was feeling extremely drained as I skirted over some climbs at the edge of the great divide. Torn between Coonabarabran and Narrabri, I had to call it a day after a measly 160 km. “Ain't nothing between here and Narrabri but squashed wombat”, the proprietor at the Coonabarabran Hotel had advised. Considering the almost non-existent population in the outback, I was surprised to see a large number of rubbish in addition to the road kill. Particularly surprising was the large amount of discarded ‘adult’ magazines. There is still a market for lonely truckers who lack internet connection.

I was stoked to have enjoyed the full range of Aussie wildlife. I had seen numerous emu families, mobs of kangaroos and wombats (sadly most of them squashed). Various lizards and large snakes often scampered or slithered across the road. The bird life was colourful. The squawking call of the cockatoos sounded similar to me throwing a bike tantrum.

Australian magpies, however, were one bird I did not enjoy. These hateful creatures had been attacking me since Perth, but on this day they were particularly savage. I felt like I was riding in the Alfred Hitchcock movie 'The Birds'. Like their sports teams, Australian magpies don't play by the rules. Way more aggressive than their kin in New Zealand, they attack cowardly from behind, deliberately picking the times when a 48-wheel road train is bearing down on you.

Apart from the morons in the West Wyalong Hotel, our cuzzies from over the ditch were really good to me and I was hosted by some truly welcoming Australian families. The last to host me was in the depressing town of Moree, notorious for its crime and aboriginal alcoholism. Hayden (originally a kiwi) and his wife had seven children, the oldest no more than 12. They rented a small three bedroom house on the edge of town and had little to spare. They happily moved the kids to the living room to make room for me, fed me, and fully supported my trip. They made their strong Christian beliefs clear on their Warm Showers profile, stating that unmarried couples would not be hosted. Their house, however, had the most amazing atmosphere of love and kindness. These kids were home-schooled and had limited access to technology. Instead, they drew pictures, did their homework and played; caring and sharing with each other in the garden. Yet another 'meant to be' moment.

My second to last day in Australia I crossed into Queensland for a long and isolated slog to the town of Millmerran, where I stayed in a cabin at the Caravan Park. The proprietors had heard all about my journey, from Jennie, as she booked it. Their daughter had recently died of cancer...they gave me a free room. Tears.

The final day in Australia was to be a bitch. Throughout the journey I came realise that the joy or stress of cycling depends on seven specific stressors. Traffic, road surface, hills, navigation, mechanical issues, weather and wind (although wind is linked to weather, its influence is huge and therefore it gets its own category). It was to be my last day outside New Zealand and it seemed only fair that I should get a good sized sample of each stressor. The closer I was getting to home, the harder I was getting hit.

I started out with a head wind and a few hills, on a heavily chipped road, to Toowoomba. In the afternoon heat I punctured twice in close succession, both on the main highway. The Battle of Brisbane began, with confusing suburbs and short sharp hills leading towards a busy centre. This was followed by dangerous shoulder-less city roads. Brisbane was bustling! Friday night fever had begun. It was as though I just needed to be kicked one last time, purely for spite. Barring disaster, I had known for a few days now that I should beat the record, but I wasn't getting out easy. My last day outside New Zealand was a killer.

Matthew Bigg's sister Karen had been an avid follower of my trip from the start. She was waiting to meet me and had made plans that made my transition in and out of Brisbane a breeze. She had a hotel room booked for me, right next to the airport; she readied pizza, pasta, and organised transfers. We had a meal, shared laughs and made fun of her brother. More kindness from an old friend.

Crossing the Nullarbor, artist's impression
By Andrew Nicholson

Chapter 14

New Zealand

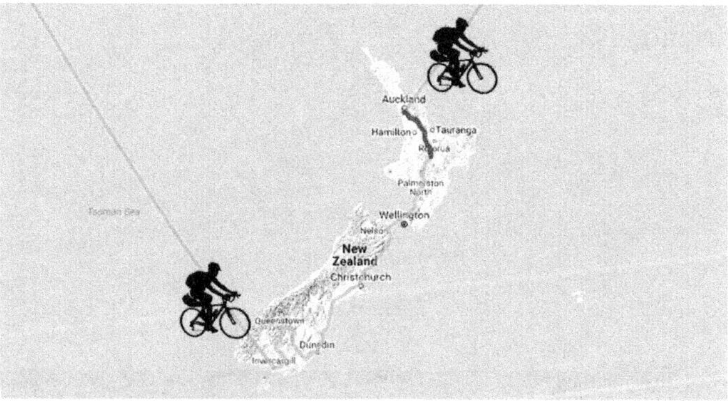

I would spend Day 118 getting to New Zealand and would arrive in Invercargill that evening. It was only 230 km from my home, but I still needed to ride another 1,600 km on an indirect route to Auckland. I needed to ensure I had some buffer kilometres on the record, in case Guinness should find and decide to subtract any westerly movements. By Chris's calculations I would finish with 29,209 km. I had hoped to enjoy a comfortable victory roll to the finish and was willing for strong southerlies. I would not be so lucky, the forecast looked nasty. My massive days across Australia had me ahead of the record but I couldn't muck about. Besides, I obviously wanted to finish as fast as possible.

I touched down at Wellington Airport where I conducted a TV interview before I made my transfer to Invercargill. There was no media scrum. A solo cameraman/reporter, who hadn't done any homework on my journey, showed up and seemed disinterested. I updated him on the basic facts. He said they might put something on the next night.

In Invercargill, I was met by family of my old skating friend, Ken Howie. Ken's brother led me a couple of kilometres to their Mum's house. Eunice had hosted me way back in 1991 when I rode the Tour of Southland. She tended to me in a kind grandmotherly way, serving up large portions of home cooked food which I greedily devoured. It seemed ironic that 25 years after my first Tour of Southland I was staying in the very same house, but on a very different cycle tour. I woke to a huge feast of bacon and eggs before heading out into rain, only stopping briefly at the SIT Velodrome for an interview with the Southland Times.

I headed Northeast. By now I had stripped my kit down to next to nothing in a bid to save weight, and I was freezing. I had acclimatised to the heat of Australia and although it was summer, this was Southland. I should have known better. With little more than a thin rain jacket I was soon shivering, grumpy, alone and battling a headwind. Some welcome home. Riding on the back roads north of Invercargill bought back from memories of the Tour of Southland, back in normal racing days.

Back then, at race pace, it was never long before a short stage finish had you warming up again in a van or hotel. But despite having had a day on a plane I had hardly recovered. I was going slower than ever now, and there was no such thing as a quick burst.

I thought back to the previous time I had travelled along this road. I had done a training run six months earlier. Portobello-Balclutha-Owaka-Catlin's Coast and home via Gore, 400 km. On that occasion I'd averaged nearly 30kph. It was one of those small rides that contributed to this massive one. Today I was barely averaging 20 and couldn't go any faster. Given the circumstances, I hardly felt like a world record breaking cyclist. I trudged into Mataura then on to Gore, getting increasingly cold and grumpy.

I stopped to warm up in the Gore KFC. After a couple of quarter packs, my hands had stopped shaking enough to operate my phone. Closing in on the finish I went online, curious as to how much money my trip had raised for cancer research. Even if my ride was successful I didn't expect a great deal of actual cash donations. But given that there had been a couple of online articles, and that my story may have been on tele, I had hoped for something. I checked the total.

I was disappointed. I then learned that my tele story had been bumped. Already in a foul mood, the news caused me to fly into an online rage, via a ranting Facebook post. I was pissed off!! And I let it known on my page. I threatened to stop at Dunedin, I was done! As far as I was concerned, I had done my lap. Nobody would care if the record was official or not. I pointed out that a former Silver Fern could push a pram in a 5 km fun run and get more attention. I added correctly that fat former All Blacks would raise 10 times this amount of money, by jumping into the ring for a 3-minute charity fight. For Christ sake, I was about to break a world record for the toughest endurance challenge imaginable! I'd put myself through hell, for a cause that affects so many people, and no one gave a shit! I remounted and I plodded toward Lumsden, telling myself that I would finish tomorrow in Dunedin and stay at home. I was done! Fuck the record!

A couple of hours later, the wind dropped as I turned north toward Queenstown. The rain cleared and I had a spectacular mountain view of the aptly named Remarkables, reflecting perfectly off Lake Wakatipu. Something was different about the air? I could breathe? I hadn't tasted air this clean for months. I rode over a stream, looking down at the crystal clear water, I could see the bottom? Apart from my first couple of days in the Rocky Mountains, I hadn't seen water so clear since my departure. In the past 115 days I had crossed nothing but stagnant and sludge filled waterways.

The road was quiet. There was no traffic, no blasting horns, no diesel fumes clogging my lungs. There was no rubbish piled up on the roadside, just sheep grazing on the green slopes of the mountain valley floor. I immediately remembered what I had come home to. Suddenly I felt a rush of guilt about my online tantrum.

I may have had a very valid point, but there was a handful of very special people who *had* supported me, from the start. My Facebook following was small, but it had grown as my trip progressed. People I'd never met had joined in, and some had made donations. Then there were my Warm Showers hosts, who not only supported me, but sent numerous messages of encouragement. In bleak moments in Indian or Turkish hotels, these Facebook comments had meant a lot to me. There were people like Paco in Spain, Heather and Judith, cancer sufferers who hosted me in Australia, strangers who willingly helped. I considered my skating teammates who had contributed to this quest. I thought of my brother and Tanis, who had joined mission control helping with the online coordinating of numerous jobs for which I had no longer had the time or brainpower to complete. Then there were Jennie and Marcela, who had dealt with my sometimes irrational online behaviour right from Day 1. They had put in countless hours; coordinating hosts, hotels, air tickets and often stayed up to unthinkable hours, nervously tracking me, praying that I would safely arrive at my proposed destination. No way could I stop. Their support plus the paradise I was now riding through was a reminder to be grateful. I felt incredibly guilty. Approaching Queenstown, I picked up internet coverage. There were several messages urging me to continue. One in particular stood out, a stranger wrote:

> ***Markus*** *Andrew, you've done something truly amazing. I have started cycling around the world myself, on a single speed bike and self-supported. I took a break to wish my father goodbye, who has died after a bike accident on Thursday, and will be back on the bike next week in the US. I have followed your journey throughout, and can fully understand how you are feeling. Don't let your anger about a lack of media coverage or donations spoil what you have achieved. I am sure there have been many people that have helped you getting where you are, ride for them. I have worked many years in marketing and PR, two of those in New Zealand. People do not appreciate what you have achieved by the looks of it, but those people following here do. Get on that bike and ride again. Deal with the PR afterwards, the impact you've made on the people following here is greater than a few*

moments of fame on local radio and TV. I have always tried to generate interest for my trips, but I couldn't be bothered this time, as some journalists simply didn't get it. They are mainly not interested in good news and dig deeper into what it means to ride like this. Stay positive, I hope you cross that line soon.

I don't know if I ever would have stopped. I do know my story and the cause behind it certainly deserved a great deal more exposure, but I continued to feel I had been selfish through my comments. Truth is, Tanty was tired and upset. Like a toddler, I had thrown a tantrum for attention, and I got it. Over the next few hours there was a spike in donations. My rage was a slight protest about how, sometimes, the recognition of an achievement is dictated by the media rather than by the scale of the achievement. It is dictated by how you look, what sells, and whether you and your sport are marketable. What I was doing was an epic achievement in aid of a major cause. I was about to break another World Record. 235 kilometres a day, every day, non-stop! Over 29,000 kilometres, mostly unsupported. I did have a point...but still, I wouldn't stop.

Ken Howie drove down from Queenstown, guided me to his home and cheered me up. Another link to skating, making this trip possible. I awoke to more encouragement online and left Queenstown in a better mood, with stunning New Zealand mountain vistas surrounding me. But the wind picked up and a strong easterly had me ranting again, as I slogged through the Cromwell Gorge.

Chris contacted some friends of his who were training near Alexandra, they met and guided me to a cafe and fed me up on kiwi pies. They were encouraging, welcome company, and in awe of my trip. With a stomach full of mince and cheese pie I felt better, but within 10 minutes of leaving Alexandra I hit nasty climbs and a powerful headwind. The tantrum metre hit maximum and I began yet another crazy-man rage. At times throughout the day I simply stopped and lay down in the gutter, momentarily breaking down. I just didn't want to ride anymore.

Approaching Highway 1, a Facebook fan Steve and his family were parked by the roadside. They had driven out from Dunedin to meet me. Steve had been posting a trade mark *'Whoop Whoop'* war cry comment on My Facebook page throughout my journey. His family cheered and clapped as I approached. *'WHOOP! WHOOP! keep going!'* read the large sign they held and waved at me. I finally turned North and the wind swung around. In the rural town of Milton my convoy would increase. Parked at the side of the road was my own car, with Marcela smiling beside it. I hadn't seen her since she dumped me in the outback, over two weeks earlier. I stopped for a long and emotional embrace.

Steve Dyet from AvantiPlus had also come out to shake my hand and offer support. A couple of local riders joined in and kept me company for the final 60 km to my home city. With even the wind having obliged by briefly turning to my back, I was riding on a high. Talk about an emotional rollercoaster. Only one hour earlier I had been lying in a ditch groaning and screaming at the wind gods.

I rode through Mosgiel and dropped down into my home city of Dunedin. I was home! But I wasn't finished. Every night, for nearly four months, I'd slept in a different bed. Tonight I would sleep with Marcela beside me and in my own bed. Seven hours later I had to go back to the front. I still needed to ride 1,250 km to Auckland, and as quick as possible.

Word of my arrival got out and I was pleased to wake to a reception of local riders and supporters, who turned out for an informal welcome at the harbour front. I gave a short speech about my journey, elicited some laughs and thanked everyone for coming down. Again, no media scrum. I gave a positive account of my trip to the one reporter from the Otago Daily Times, but his write up was negative, focusing mostly on my Facebook rant. I should have known better. The AvantiPlus crew and a dozen or so riders followed me over the large climb heading north, and with company, the time flew by. My entourage turned back and later that morning I shared a precious 15 minute picnic at Palmerston with Marcela, before she returned to work. I continued north.

Alone again, a strong northerly picked up after Oamaru. The dial on the tantrum metre immediately swung back into the red. I was done with headwinds! *"GIVE ME A FUCKING BREAK!!"* I bellowed at full strength, struggling along at no more than 20 kph, *"FUCK OFF, FUCK YOU!"*... I lacked the energy to be more creative with my expletives. I turned and noticed a rider on my wheel. His name was Brian. I was massively embarrassed, knowing Brian must have heard my latest outburst. Brian had been tracking me, and he was training for the upcoming Tour de Aotearoa mountain bike brevet. Brian revealed his own bicycle tantrum tendencies and I felt less ashamed, perhaps I wasn't so weird. He treated me to a much needed feed of Chinese takeaways, before heading back to Timaru. Tanis had organised a bed for me, with friends in Orari further on. I collapsed in a typical rural Kiwi farmhouse with kind strangers.

Day 119 began with a mere two hours of peace before a strong warm Norwester picked up on the Canterbury plains. I skirted Christchurch, over some damaged roads that had yet to be fixed since the devastating 2011 earthquake. A couple of hours north of the city, a friendly looking young woman waved me down from the roadside, while pulling a mountain bike off her car's bike rack. She introduced herself as Rita, she had heard about my trip, and she wanted to ride with me. Rita was lovely, I appreciated the support and enthusiasm;

but I was still in a race for a world record and I couldn't slow down to talk to girls on mountain bikes. But Rita was having no trouble keeping up with me, and it soon became clear why. She had recently ridden for New Zealand in the Commonwealth Games. In fact, I was struggling to hold conversation up the hills, and if we had started racing, she would have dropped me.

In spite of the achievement, things were still being done in a minimalist fashion. Hotels were still a last resort, and just like my early skating trips, it was still about 'who do we know that can put me up?' Tanis had organised yet another wonderful couple named Greg and Bev, who lived on an idyllic farm near Cheviot. Another day, another 265 km.

After an early start, a puncture and a couple of nasty climbs, I was riding along the familiar Kaikoura coast. I had the vast blue Pacific Ocean on my right and the steep snow-capped Kaikoura mountains on my left, it was New Zealand scenery at its best. A familiar rider approached. It was Chris Nicholson! New Zealand's toughest ever athlete. It seemed fitting as I neared the end of my journey that I would reunite with the person who was the greatest inspiration behind it.

The people we surround ourselves with either

raise or lower our standards. They either help us to become the best versions of ourselves, or encourage us to become lesser versions of ourselves. We become like the friends we have chosen and the people we follow. We all need people in our lives to raise our standards and remind us of what it takes to be the best we can be. In spite of all the disadvantages I faced as a young skater, I was extremely lucky to have my brother as a role model. Back then of course I just thought he was a dick.

From the moment Chris got his first pair of speed skates and racing bike, he led a life of 100% commitment to his goals. If he wasn't sleeping, eating or working, he was training, and training hard. Very early on Chris had helped me ingrain the necessary habits of a champion and those required to fulfil my Olympic dream.

In 1987 Chris had a freak and serious skating accident in Christchurch. Most crashes in short track speed skating end without incident. The barriers are well padded. A crash might knock the wind or pride out of you but usually that's about it. Not so this day, it would literally knock the shit out of my brother Chris.

Short track speed skates are long and extremely sharp. They protrude a full 10 centimetres in front and behind the boot. In a time trial, Chris fell. His skate became caught awkwardly beneath him as he ploughed into the barrier. The entire force of his body followed through on the heel of his blade, perforating and tearing apart his bowel. Blood and other bodily fluids covered the ice. Chris was in agony and conscious throughout, by all accounts it was a horrific scene. While an ambulance was rushed to the scene Chris was moved onto one of the safety mats for warmth. After a long stay in hospital Chris was fitted with a colostomy bag. He took a brief break from the ice and was soon racing his bike, still connected to the colostomy bag.

Nobody ever bothered do a decent job of removing the stains on the crash mat after Chris's crash. In the following years, Chris would return to the ice and skate thousands of laps past what would become known as 'the bowel perforation mat'. One would think that such a visual reminder would deter you from ever skating again but Chris was soon back on the ice doing lap after lap past the remains of his entrails.

Chris Nicholson is without doubt one of New Zealand's toughest athletes ever. He would go on to break more of both bones and records. Over the years he would become a world speed skating champion and twice New Zealand Cycling Champion, both in the road race and time trial. He would become New Zealand's only male winter and summer Olympian. He would go on to have a lengthy career in cycling and get up from several more serious cycling and skating accidents.

In 2013 he bounced back from a heart

complication and cardiac arrest. Months later he was racing at an elite level, aged 48. Never was he placing his sporting projects ahead of his family. Today Chris provides a huge amount of support and mentoring for Nelson Cycling. A true and humble champion. Without Chris Nicholson as a role model I would never have had a chance.

I once read a Kiwi sports book called 'Hard Men Fight Back'. Except for Multisport legend Steve Gurney, I was not overly impressed. The book was generally about recovering alcoholics, violent rugby players and various others who had gone bad but apparently turned good in the end. I question the way we use those who 'did bad but came good' as role models. Should we not show more respect for those who had the self-control and discipline to stay on track in the first place? They didn't need to go bad to become good. Chris Nicholson was ten times tougher and dedicated than any off the rails All Black, he had the self-discipline and respect for himself to stay on track in the first place.

Chris slowed to swing around but the traffic was busy, many people were heading for the AC/DC concert in Wellington. Rather than stop and wait for a brotherly reunion, I attacked! I knew Chris would find this amusing. I also knew it wouldn't be long before he would catch me. This delay gave a me few hundred metres gap, which he closed within minutes. We chatted at full speed while riding and the afternoon flew by. The strangeness was gone, it like I was on just another training ride with my hero, cycling together as we had for over 30 years.

A brief but welcome break from the road.
Chris and Andrew Nicholson share lunch.

My sister in law Jenny drove out, took some great photos, and led Chris and I to Blenheim Airport. I would take a 20 minute hop across the Cook Strait on a ten seater plane. Not only was the flight a freebee, courtesy of Sounds Air, it meant I could avoid the awkward battle of Wellington. I landed in the North Island slightly north of Wellington, at Kapati airfield, my second antipodal point. Dig a hole straight through the Earth and I would come out near Paco's place, in Spain. I continued riding around 60 km to Levin. The proprietors of the Levin Travelodge were fighting their own cancer battle, cancer sufferer number seven. They had heard about my trip and sponsored me the night.

550 km to ride and two days to go. I woke to a strong northerly, it wasn't fair! I had had headwinds ever since Invercargill. I climbed out from Taihape to over 1,000m, on to the Desert Road. The volcanic peaks of the North Island mountains occasionally appeared in gaps in the clouds to my left. By the time I hit Waiouru my average was pitiful, an all-time low of 21 kph. It was cold, windy, wet and miserable, but I wasn't the first world circumnavigation rider to struggle on this stretch of road. In 2010, a hypothermic Juliana Buhring had needed to be rescued here by a passing campervan in 100kph winds, manly points! Finally I descended to Taupo. My final hosts, Peter and Anne, met me at their holiday home. The same couple had sent out their friends to find me and offer support, back on Day 7 in Moose Jaw.

My final day, and just for a change I woke to heavy rain, and a headwind. This wasn't fair! I let rip with one final rant. I had earned this record, for god's sake just blow me home. Realising however that I was about to break a world record, it was only right that things should be difficult. If I had had an easy finish, it would have made the record feel less deserved. I shouldn't want it to be easy. Perhaps it was only fair that I should struggle for one last day. The greater the struggle, the greater the sense of achievement.

In Matamata (also known for the Lord of the Rings village of Hobbiton) I was met by an old friend and personal training client. I'd met Dave in 2003, when he was an out of shape, overweight anaesthetist, with a bunch of cash but a body in need of serious attention. I had inspired Dave to make some changes and he had made the effort. A couple of years later Dave had finished the one day Coast to Coast event. I hoped my trip would inspire others to also appreciate that your health is your greatest asset. Without a healthy and fit body, adventures are limited.

My Dad had driven out from Whitianga to see me finish, ironically he met me on the exact same road where Paul had set the original NGF record. The traffic was thick and the chip heavy on this notoriously dangerous stretch of highway, but with only two hours to go, I was done with throwing tantrums. I was even starting to smile, in spite of the conditions.

So close now! I climbed up the Bombay Hill. This final hill was considered a tough climb as kid. Now, compared to some of the mountains I had climbed in the last four months, it seemed like a tiddler. The large city of Auckland spread out below me, 20 kilometres to go! I dropped down onto Great South Road, where Sunday bunch rides began for me, as a teenager. The sets of traffic lights had tripled since then, but there was no rage. I was nearly done. I turned left towards airport.

One kilometre out, I stopped to take a final picture of my bike next to the Auckland International Airport sign. A tall, familiar figure came loping towards me, cheering and frantically ringing a large bell. It was Mike McMillen! Mike had borrowed the bell from the skating club, the same bell that had been used to indicate the final lap in numerous skating races. If a kilometre were to signify a lap, then this was indeed the very last. 29,2008 done, one to go. Mike high fived me, joking that there had been a mix up with the lap counting and that I would have to go around again to be sure, hence the bell.

Mike whipped back to the official finish line leaving me alone to complete the final kilometre. Emotion swept over me as I entered the final 200 metres, passing a long rank of taxis. At the finish line, a small group had gathered and all were cheering by the AvantiPlus finish line. I could hear the bell, still being rung enthusiastically by Mike. The waiting taxi drivers, who had no idea what was happening, heard the commotion and stepped out to join in the clapping. The crowd was three times bigger than when I left, about 20 (not counting the taxi drivers). It was mostly made up of members of the Hauraki speed skating club. It was small group but included some very special people. My Dad, Mike, Igor, Tony Smith and Jennie. My front wheel gently dropped over the speed bump which signified the finish line. I clipped out of the pedals for the last time.

A TV reporter and cameraman had shown up to record the moment. I was interviewed moments after I finished, and when asked what memorable moments stood out, I stared, dumbstruck. I couldn't even think of a clear answer. There had simply been too many.

Done! 20,209 km. Jennie acts as sound crew for TVNZ

We had a small gathering at a nearby airport hotel, where my Dad had organised a room for the night. After a few celebration drinks, the small group dispersed and it was time to sleep.

It would be yet another day before I'd get my first proper sleep in. I needed to get up at 5:00am for a TV Breakfast Show interview. I went to my room still in my bike gear, I hadn't even had a chance to wash. I took off my bike kit for the last time, turned on the tap and stepped into the shower. Relaxing a moment too soon, I stretched for the soap. My feet disappeared from under me on the slippery bathroom floor and I went down, hard! Too slow and too weak to get my hands in any position to protect myself, I collapsed with loud *thunk*. My ribs were badly bruised and my elbow clearly needed stitching. I was hurt! Grandpa had had a fall in the shower.

For four months I had ridden through madness, and had come away virtually unscathed. I had cycled in a state of constant fatigue, bombarded with all the stressors of cycling. I'd ridden through the madness of Indian traffic and avoided thousands of potholes; I'd evaded cholera, dysentery and bush fires. I had made it through deadly mountain descents, dog attacks, floods; I narrowly avoided a bombing in Turkey and survived the suicidal drivers of Eastern Europe. But now that I was home, reaching for the soap in the shower had been an act too far. I had clearly emptied the tank.

My dad had already fallen asleep but the fall had woken him. I played down my injury. The stitching could wait, I didn't care. I wrapped the wound in a hotel towel and fell asleep with a proud grin on my face. I'd done it!

After my interview Jennie drove me to a medical centre near my old ice rink where my elbow was properly stitched. She then dropped me back to the airport for my flight home to Dunedin. I bought her some flowers and hugged her goodbye. Dozens of people helped make my achievement possible but Jennie had been the most significant helper. She alone would have easily saved me more than the scant 52 hours by which I had beaten the record.

Flying home, I looked down at our small country, trying to pick out the various towns. What I assumed was Blenheim, upon closer inspection turned out to be Christchurch. That's it? That's the biggest city in this whole island? I'd been through dozens of cities like this in a few blinks. Although I have always had a clear perspective of the size of the planet, traveling the whole planet by bicycle made it even clearer. Travelling by bicycle gives you a real sense of population and distance. You don't travel on planes or in cars, you get teleported. Travelling in motorised transport is like watching a movie, but on a bike, you're actually in the movie.

Epilogue

People ask if I kept a diary, the answer is no. I did keep a scrappy log book for key facts and numbers as required by Guinness, but there was no time for a detailed writing journal, there was no need. I remember every moment and have had no trouble recalling them for this book. I remember it all; the good, the bad and the ugly. I remember being soaked in the rain in the dark, after five punctures, at the end of a day of navigational nightmares in Bremen. I remember the more glorious moments. Descending through valleys of the Canadian Rockies, or bright red Australian outback sunsets. Nature at its best. I remember the people, all my hosts, the madness of Indian roads and terrifying thunderstorms in Thailand. I remember everything! I certainly don't remember the more routine days of my life of which fortunately there have been few.

When I was working in Coventry, UK in 2010, I was planning to return to New Zealand and enter another Coast to Coast. To prepare, I joined the Coventry Canoe Club where I got to know a guy named Mike. Mike was a mad keen paddler. Religiously on Tuesdays, Thursdays and Saturdays we would paddle, as he had for 20 years, through the wheelie bins, supermarket trolleys and traffic cones bobbing in the grungy green canal.

Mike's passion for kayaking had kept him fit. He had previously raced throughout Britain and in Europe. His life had certainly been more adventurous than the average Brit, but now he had been in one place and in the same job for a long, long time. We discussed the concept of time and its seemingly accelerating speed as we age. "It's all one long blur to me", Mike had said. By contrast I can pinpoint, almost to the day, where I was over the past 30 years. I don't think it's because I have an exceptional memory. I think it is because my life has been one long series of ambitious goals and travel projects. A life full of memorable moments.

Upon return, Jennie helped me compile and submit the huge amount of evidence required to make my record official. This arduous task took as long as my ride but in July my application was approved! I am now officially the fastest man to cycle around the world. Sadly we just missed the deadline to make the 2017 printed edition of the Guinness Book of Records. Hopefully a full year will pass before my record is beaten and I will see my name for a third time in this fascinating book.

I have not had an easy transition back to the real world. I have received several more *'Thank you, but there was a high standard of applicants...'* rejection letters, for teaching jobs and on November 3 my teacher's registration expired. Teachers who have not completed sufficient hours in full time positions are now required to retrain, at a cost of $4000, to maintain registration.

Given that I have been rejected for innumerable full time positions for seven years now, I have opted out. I get angry about this at times but I know it's not me. Sadly, everyone including New Zealand's children, loses because of the lack foresight of principals and board members who prefer to go with the 'status quo' teacher.

I am still working part time at the gym until I can find a more meaningful future. My shoulder aches from a recent ice hockey accident and I await an operation. I paint and occasionally sell watercolours, this may be a potential avenue for me, I have a included a couple of pictures in this book. Watercolour painting is certainly less physically taxing than racing around the world by bicycle and I never have tantrums. I find it a relaxing and peaceful activity.

My gym instructor shifts are not challenging. I clean the machines while most gym goers strut by like peacocks, too arrogant to utilise the services on offer. The Olympic and Guinness World Record certificate I hung on the gym wall meant little to the average punter playing on the equipment. I have taken them home where they belong. I get told that the music is shit, and to switch the TV channel. I smile and keep the public happy on the rare occasions when they ask for exercise advice.

Recently a rude, fat woman wobbled past me as I was finishing off mopping the floor. She attempted to cast her towel into the 'used' bucket of gym towels but her throw was weak. The towel landed directly on my outstretched arm. Fortunately, the latest edition of 'Woman's Day' had kept Jabba from working up too much of a sweat. She waddled away without apology, but I didn't really notice this disrespectful act. My mind had been elsewhere. I'd been in Zambia.

The same morning I had finished the book 'Africa Solo' by Mark Beaumont, the legendary ultra-cyclist who had previously held my record. In 2015. Mark had set an impressive 41-day world record, averaging 260 km from Cairo to Cape Town. He had battled the usual challenges of heat, wind, rain, hostile locals and other hazards that only a handful of ultra-cyclists on the planet can relate to.

The Cape Town - Cairo record perhaps? I threw the idea of attempting the African record at Lester. His response - "Do you need to break yet another world record? Why not just enjoy Africa at sensible pace?" He had a point. The ability to break the record is probably still there, but for the moment the money certainly isn't. Besides, how far does one push one's luck? I don't need to prove anything by breaking another world record, but I will certainly cycle in Africa one day, probably selected areas, with Marcela. Several Warm Showers guests Marcela and I have hosted since my return have also served as reminders that there is no need to race.

I also recently finished reading Juliana Buhring's book - 'This Road I Ride'. Her inspirational circumnavigation story defines courage and adventure. Her book also largely enabled me to relive my own journey, Juliana motivated to me to continue with at least some sort of travel project.

I had liaised briefly with Juliana both before and after my ride. Juliana had also struggled with adjusting from life on the road, and she wrote to me *"...planning the next adventure, even the smallest, will help to make the transition easier"*.

So true, without adventure life will pass you by.

Statistics

Started:	12 August 2015
Duration:	123 Days & 43 mins
Distance Cycled:	29,209km
Countries Passed Through:	23
Number of Punctures:	47
Number of Tyres Used:	8
Number of Chains Used:	3
Crashes:	2
Number of Tantrums:	Too many to count
Finished:	13 December 2015

Daily Log

Day	Country	City	Km's
1	Canada	Abbotsford	76
2	Canada	Princeton	222
3	Canada	Kelowna	178
4	Canada	Revelstoke	207
5	Canada	Canmore	327
6	Canada	Calgary	116
7	Canada	Medicine Hat	325
8	Canada	Swift Current	250
9	Canada	Moose Jaw	188
10	Canada	Kola	395
11	Canada	Killarney	245
12	USA	Thief River Falls	384
13	USA	Brainerd	337
14	USA	Luck	269
15	USA	Galesville	268
16	USA	Madison	278
17	USA	Streamwood	201
18	USA	South Bend	214
19	USA	Toledo	264
20	USA	Mentor	256
21	USA	Lancaster NY	308
22	USA	Syracuse	254
23	USA	Mohawk	123
24	USA	Albany	198
25	USA	Hartford	247
26	USA	Boston	203
27	Flight to Portugal		
28	Portugal	Redondo	202
29	Portugal	Covilha	261
30	Spain	Medina del campo	314
31	Spain	Burgos	222

Day	Country	City	Km's
32	Spain	San Sebastian	256
33	Spain	San Sebastian	
34	France	Bordeaux	253
35	France	La Rochelle	221
36	France	Nantes	149
37	France	Blois	299
38	France	Auxerre	234
39	France	Nancy	281
40	Holland	Aachen	297
41	Holland	Rotterdam	238
42	Holland	Assen	220
43	Germany	Achim	211
44	Germany	Hildesheim	141
45	Germany	Halle (Saale)	211
46	Czech Rep.	Prague	340
47	Czech Rep.	Cizova	113
48	Czech Rep.	Brno	225
49	Hungary	Gyor	234
50	Hungary	Szeged	316
51	Serbia	Opovo	204
52	Romania	Drobeta-Turnu	295
53	Bulgaria	Vidin	124
54	Bulgaria	Troyan	287
55	Bulgaria	Svilengrad	261
56	Turkey	Galipoli	230
57	Turkey	Bursa	248
58	Turkey	Sivrihisar	302
59	Turkey	Ankara	159
60	Turkey	Cankiri	184
61	Turkey	Inebolu	193
62	Turkey	Gerze	174
63	Turkey	Fatsa	242
64	Turkey	Trabzon	274

Day	Country	City	Km's
65	Turkey	Hopa	174
66	Georgia	Samtredia	186
67	Georgia	Gori	184
68	Georgia	Tbilisi	82
69	Georgia	Tbilisi Airport	20
70	India	Naygaon	163
71	India	Karad	209
72	India	Solapur	223
73	India	Zaheerabad	238
74	India	Koyalagudem	166
75	India	Vijayawada	215
76	India	Rajahmundry	218
77	India	Visakhapatnum	248
78	India	Brahmapur	269
79	India	Cuttack	227
80	India	Balasore	198
81	India	Kolkata	270
82	Thailand	Flight to Bangkok / Chiang Mai	
83	Thailand	Lampang	104
84	Thailand	Nakhon Sawan	398
85	Thailand	Ratchaburi	319
86	Thailand	Prachuap Khiri Khan	280
87	Thailand	Chang Wat Chumphon	225
88	Thailand	Nakhon Si Thammarat	314
89	Thailand	Chang Wat	273
90	Malaysia	Taiping	256
91	Malaysia	Kuala Selangor	243
92	Malaysia	Muar	290
93	Singapore	Changi Airport	219
94	Australia	Crossman	120
95	Australia	Kalgan	337
96	Australia	Jerdacuttup	328
97	Australia	Salmon Gums	324

Day	Country	City	Km's
98	Australia	Balladonia	338
99	Australia	Mundrabilla	328
100	Australia	Border Village	304
101	Australia	Merghiny	390
102	Australia	Solomon	304
103	Australia	Wilmington	241
104	Australia	Adelaide	321
105	Australia	Keith	245
106	Australia	Dartmoor	272
107	Australia	Port Campbell	236
108	Australia	Melbourne	292
109	Australia	Shepparton	256
110	Australia	Albury	181
111	Australia	West Wyalong	314
112	Australia	Dubbo	287
113	Australia	Coonabarabran	171
114	Australia	Moree	239
115	Australia	Millmerran	296
116	Australia	Brisbane	243
117	New Zealand	Flight to Invercargill	
118	New Zealand	Queenstown	258
119	New Zealand	Dunedin	299
120	New Zealand	Orari	259
121	New Zealand	Spotswood	264
122	New Zealand	Levin	230
123	New Zealand	Taupo	283
124	New Zealand	Auckland	290

Notes

1. loseb Besarionis dze Jughashvili https://en.wikipedia.org/wiki/Joseph_Stalin#Early_life.
2. Guinness World Records Specific Guidelines Document "**Fastest circumnavigation by bicycle (male)**"
3. Roald Amundsen Telegram https://en.wikiquote.org/wiki/Roald_Amundsen
4. Golubac Fortress https://en.wikipedia.org/wiki/Golubac_Fortress
5. Bombing in Ankara https://en.wikipedia.org/wiki/2015_Ankara_bombings
6. Battle of Sinop https://en.wikipedia.org/wiki/Battle_of_Sinop
7. Burma Railway https://en.wikipedia.org/wiki/Burma_Railway#Prisoners_of_War
8. Nullarbor Plain https://en.wikipedia.org/wiki/Nullarbor_Plain
9. Ferninand Magellan https://en.wikipedia.org/wiki/Ferdinand_Magellan#Voyage_of_circumnavigation

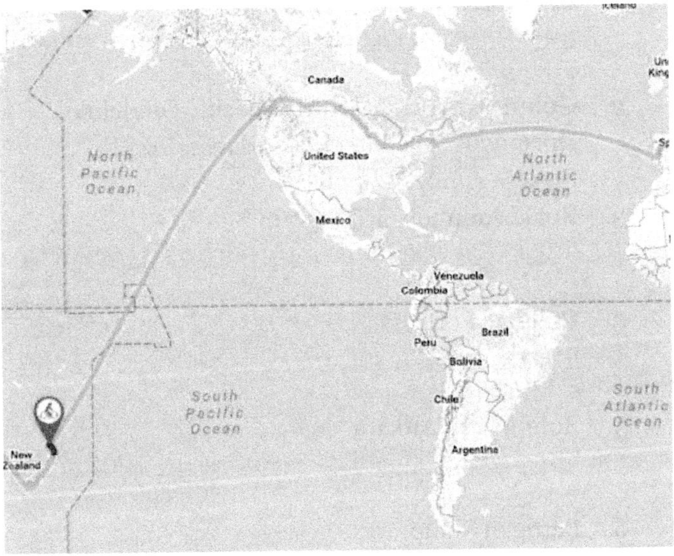
Canada
United States
North Pacific Ocean
North Atlantic Ocean
Mexico
Venezuela
Colombia
Brazil
Peru
Bolivia
Chile
Argentina
South Pacific Ocean
South Atlantic Ocean
New Zealand

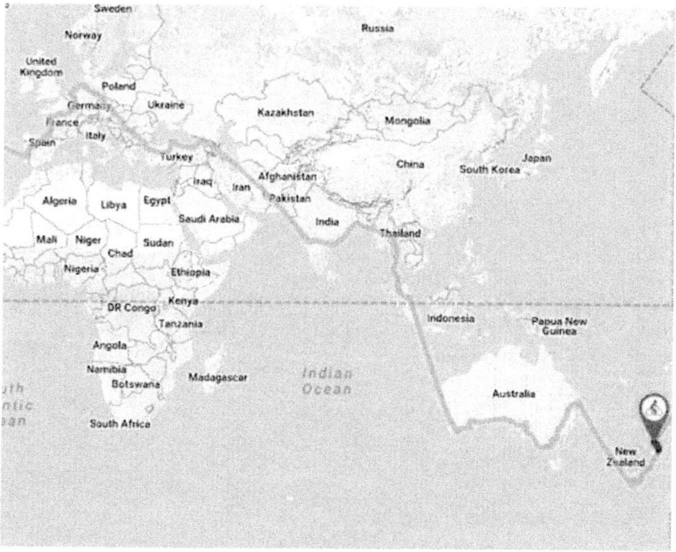
Sweden
Norway
Russia
United Kingdom
Poland
Germany
Ukraine
Kazakhstan
Mongolia
France
Italy
Spain
Turkey
China
South Korea
Japan
Iraq
Iran
Afghanistan
Pakistan
Algeria
Libya
Egypt
Saudi Arabia
India
Mali
Niger
Chad
Sudan
Thailand
Nigeria
Ethiopia
Kenya
DR Congo
Tanzania
Indonesia
Papua New Guinea
Angola
Namibia
Botswana
Madagascar
Indian Ocean
Australia
South Africa
New Zealand

Made in the
USA
Middletown, DE

76802042R00179